ORGANIZING CRIME

The Mystery Company's Guide to Series

edited by
Austin Lugar & ~~Jim Huang~~

To Chuck,
Thanks for being
such a supportive
friend.
Aust
Lyn

For (Luck,
with Thanks!
—Jim

CRUM CREEK PRESS
THE MYSTERY COMPANY
Carmel, Indiana

ACKNOWLEDGMENTS

This guide would not exist without the assistance of Jennie Jacobson, Casey Sullivan, Stephanie Warner, Miriam Guidero, Nikki Phipps, and the staff of The Mystery Company: Rebecca Hubbard, Joella Hultgren and Edna Stewart.

ORGANIZING CRIME

Copyright © 2009 by The Crum Creek Press

ISBN-10: 1-932325-09-3
ISBN-13: 978-1-932325-09-6

Cover art by Wanni Zhou
Cover design by Pat Prather

First edition: December 2009

The Crum Creek Press / The Mystery Company
484 East Carmel Drive #378
Carmel, IN 46032

www.themysterycompany.com
www.crumcreekpress.com

Introduction

Jim Huang: Hello, everyone. I've been a bookstore owner for many years now and one of the major things customers ask me is where certain books fall in their series.

Austin Lugar: You mean The Mystery Company?

Jim: What?

Austin: The store where you get questions...

Jim: What are you doing?

Austin: I just wanted to get the store's name out there. Let people know about it.

Jim: The book is called *Organizing Crime: The Mystery Company's Guide to Series Mysteries*.

Austin: So you think they know?

Jim: They know. Now we have a new book out that I think will be very helpful to all mystery fans.

Austin: All right, pitch it to me.

Jim: What? You worked on this—

Austin: I know, I'm just doing this—

Jim: Oh, for the—

Austin: Yeah, so they can—

Jim: Okay so I see where you're—

Austin: Yeah.

Jim: Right, sorry. What we did was we collected our customer's favorite active mystery series and put the books in the right canonical order.

Austin: Is that the right use of "canonical"?

Jim: Yes...

Austin: I always used that to describe things that were like a cannon.

Jim: No, that's...like what?

Austin: Like "that canonical Super Soaker injured the two-year-old with its awesome water power."

Jim: I'm in awe.

Austin: Thank you. Now what's an "active mystery series?"

Jim: It's a series where there are still regular entries and—

Austin: Hey, what's up with these boxes?

Jim: Which boxes?

Austin: (flips through the book) All of these boxes to the left of the titles.

Jim: How can you be holding a copy of the book when we're just doing the intro now?

Austin: Why are you avoiding the question?

Jim: I'm not! The boxes are whatever you want them to be.

Austin: That's a cheat.

Jim: No, it's not. You put checkmarks in them for different tasks. Like you can have the left box be "Read It" and the right box "Own It."

Austin: Or "Read It" and "Featured an Alcoholic."

Jim: I guess...

Austin: Or "Death Count Was Over 15" and "Protagonist Solved Entire Crime in Two Days."

Jim: I suppose. Again, it's all up to you.

Austin: How about "Prominently Featured Sewing" and "Solved It Before the Detective"?

Jim: Actually, I like that one. You know, people can race their friends to who can finish series first.

Austin: You know what that means?

Jim and Austin: Buying multiple copies!

Austin: Exactly. Now how about this blank line at the end of each series?

Jim: That's for you to add in new titles when new books come out.

Austin: Wait, how up to date is this?

Jim: All the books listed have been or are scheduled to be released in the United States in 2009.

Austin: So when do you think we'll update this book?

Jim: Well, we want to have it out every year.

Austin: Oh I get it. We don't want to hog all the fun. We want the readers to experience the joy of meticulously looking up each series and recording the latest entry while keeping in consideration the exact wording of the title.

Jim: ...

Austin: ...

Jim: Yes.

Austin: Now what else is in this book?

Jim: You want more?

Austin: Well, I know there is more so I feel okay about asking.

Jim: Okay then. After we finish the series, we have a collection of lists, mostly ways to find new series and recommendations.

Austin: That sounds absolutely phenomenal.

Jim: Well, I'll say it's a fun resource.

Austin: Oh, come on, Jim. I'm saying it's a beautiful book. Can I blurb that? Are we allowed to blurb our own book?

Jim: Okay, stop that. We hope everyone enjoys the book. It was a lot of fun to put together. If you find any errors or have any complaints at all please email us at Austin@TheMysteryCompany.com If you have any praise about the content or the packaging send those emails to Jim@TheMysteryCompany.com

Austin: Right. Wait...

Organizing Crime

Aird, Catherine

C.D. Sloan: This long-running series laced with comedy follows two detectives who solve crimes in and around Kent, England.

❏ ❏   #1: The Religious Body
❏ ❏   #2: Henrietta Who?
❏ ❏   #3: The Stately Home Murder
❏ ❏   #4: A Late Phoenix
❏ ❏   #5: His Burial Too
❏ ❏   #6: Slight Mourning
❏ ❏   #7: Parting Breath
❏ ❏   #8: Some Die Eloquent
❏ ❏   #9: Passing Strange
❏ ❏   #10: Last Respects
❏ ❏   #11: Harm's Way
❏ ❏   #12: A Dead Liberty
❏ ❏   #13: The Body Politic
❏ ❏   #14: A Going Concern
❏ ❏   #15: Injury Time
❏ ❏   #16: After Effects
❏ ❏   #17: Stiff News
❏ ❏   #18: Little Knell
❏ ❏   #19: Amendment of Life
❏ ❏   #20: A Hole in One
❏ ❏   #21: Losing Ground
❏ ❏   # _____

AKUNIN, BORIS

Erast Fandorin: Russia-based Fandorin is a police officer in the late 1800s.

- ❏ ❏ #1: The Winter Queen
- ❏ ❏ #2: The Turkish Gambit
- ❏ ❏ #3: Murder on the Leviathan
- ❏ ❏ #4: The Death of Achilles
- ❏ ❏ #5: Special Assignments
- ❏ ❏ # _____

Sister Pelagia: A Russian Orthodox nun located in Imperial Russia.

- ❏ ❏ #1: Sister Pelagia and the White Bulldog
- ❏ ❏ #2: Sister Pelagia and the Black Monk
- ❏ ❏ #3: Sister Pelagia and the Red Cockerel
- ❏ ❏ # _____

ALBERT, SUSAN WITTIG

Beatrix Potter: The creator of Peter Rabbit unravels mysteries with the aid of various farm animals.

- ❏ ❏ #1: The Tale of Hill Top Farm
- ❏ ❏ #2: The Tale of Holly How
- ❏ ❏ #3: The Tale of Cuckoo Brow Wood
- ❏ ❏ #4: The Tale of Hawthorn House
- ❏ ❏ #5: The Tale of Briar Bank
- ❏ ❏ # _____

China Bayles: Bayles left her life as a lawyer to live a quieter life as the owner of an herb shop in Texas.

- ❏ ❏ #1: Thyme of Death
- ❏ ❏ #2: Witches' Bane
- ❏ ❏ #3: Hangman's Root
- ❏ ❏ #4: Rosemary Remembered

❑ ❑ #5: Rueful Death
❑ ❑ #6: Love Lies Bleeding
❑ ❑ #7: Chile Death
❑ ❑ #8: Lavender Lies
❑ ❑ #9: Mistletoe Man
❑ ❑ #10: Bloodroot
❑ ❑ #11: Indigo Dying
❑ ❑ #12: A Dilly of a Death
❑ ❑ #13: Dead Man's Bones
❑ ❑ #14: Bleeding Hearts
❑ ❑ #15: Spanish Dagger
❑ ❑ #16: Nightshade
❑ ❑ #17: Wormwood
❑ ❑ # _____

ALT, MADELYN

Bewitching Mysteries: A new witch solves paranormal murders in a small town in Indiana while working at an antiques shop.
❑ ❑ #1: The Trouble With Magic
❑ ❑ #2: A Charmed Death
❑ ❑ #3: Hex Marks the Spot
❑ ❑ #4: No Rest for the Wiccan
❑ ❑ #5: Where There's a Witch There's a Way
❑ ❑ # _____

ANDREWS, DONNA

Meg Langslow: Langslow solves murders while being surrounded by zany characters and family members.
❑ ❑ #1: Murder with Peacocks
❑ ❑ #2: Murder with Puffins
❑ ❑ #3: Revenge of the Wrought-Iron Flamingos
❑ ❑ #4: Crouching Buzzard Leaping Loon

- [ ] [ ] #5: We'll Always Have Parrots
- [ ] [ ] #6: Owls Well That Ends Well
- [ ] [ ] #7: No Nest for the Wicket
- [ ] [ ] #8: The Penguin Who Knew Too Much
- [ ] [ ] #9: Cockatiels at Seven
- [ ] [ ] #10: Six Geese A-Slaying
- [ ] [ ] #11: Swan for the Money
- [ ] [ ] # _____

ARRUDA, SUZANNE

Jade del Cameron: Intrepid del Cameron investigates murders in Africa after World War I.

- [ ] [ ] #1: Mark of the Lion
- [ ] [ ] #2: Stalking Ivory
- [ ] [ ] #3: The Serpent's Daughter
- [ ] [ ] #4: The Leopard's Prey
- [ ] [ ] #5: Treasure of the Golden Cheetah
- [ ] [ ] # _____

ATHERTON, NANCY

Aunt Dimity: Despite dying many years ago, Aunt Dimity aides Lori Shephard in solving charming English mysteries.

- [ ] [ ] #1: Aunt Dimity's Death
- [ ] [ ] #2: Aunt Dimity and the Duke
- [ ] [ ] #3: Aunt Dimity's Good Deed
- [ ] [ ] #4: Aunt Dimity Digs In
- [ ] [ ] #5: Aunt Dimity's Christmas
- [ ] [ ] #6: Aunt Dimity Beats the Devil
- [ ] [ ] #7: Aunt Dimity: Detective
- [ ] [ ] #8: Aunt Dimity Takes a Holiday
- [ ] [ ] #9: Aunt Dimity Snowbound
- [ ] [ ] #10: Aunt Dimity And the Next of Kin

❑ ❑   #11: Aunt Dimity and the Deep Blue Sea
❑ ❑   #12: Aunt Dimity Goes West
❑ ❑   #13: Aunt Dimity: Vampire Hunter
❑ ❑   #14: Aunt Dimity Slays the Dragon
❑ ❑   # _____

AULT, SANDI

Wild Mysteries: Jamaica Wild works for the Bureau of
Land Management in New Mexico.

❑ ❑   #1: Wild Indigo
❑ ❑   #2: Wild Inferno
❑ ❑   #3: Wild Sorrow
❑ ❑   # _____

BAKER, DEB

Gretchen Birch: Birch restores collectible and antique
dolls.

❑ ❑   #1: Dolled Up for Murder
❑ ❑   #2: Goodbye, Dolly
❑ ❑   #3: Dolly Departed
❑ ❑   #4: Ding Dong Dead
❑ ❑   # _____

Gertie Johnson: Johnson may be 66 years old, but she
refuses to let that stop her from ironing out crimes in
Michigan's Upper Peninsula.

❑ ❑   #1: Murder Passes the Buck
❑ ❑   #2: Murder Grins And Bears It
❑ ❑   #3: Murder Talks Turkey
❑ ❑   # _____

Baldacci, David

Camel Club: Composed of four unlikely partners, the Camel Club searches for truth in Washington, DC.
- ❏ ❏ #1: The Camel Club
- ❏ ❏ #2: The Collectors
- ❏ ❏ #3: Stone Cold
- ❏ ❏ #4: Divine Justice
- ❏ ❏ # _____

Sean King: Two former Secret Service agents work as private investigators, often immersed in political affairs.
- ❏ ❏ #1: Split Second
- ❏ ❏ #2: Hour Game
- ❏ ❏ #3: Simple Genius
- ❏ ❏ #4: First Family
- ❏ ❏ # _____

Balzo, Sandra

Maggy Thorsen: In Brookhills, Wisconsin, Thorsen owns a coffee house and solves murders.
- ❏ ❏ #1: Uncommon Grounds
- ❏ ❏ #2: Grounds for Murder
- ❏ ❏ #3: Bean There, Done That
- ❏ ❏ #4: Brewed, Crude, and Tattooed
- ❏ ❏ # _____

Barnes, Linda

Carlotta Carlyle: Carlyle is a private investigator and sometime cab driver in Boston.
- ❏ ❏ #1: A Trouble of Fools
- ❏ ❏ #2: The Snake Tattoo
- ❏ ❏ #3: Coyote
- ❏ ❏ #4: Steel Guitar

❏ ❏ #5: Snapshot
❏ ❏ #6: Hardware
❏ ❏ #7: Cold Case
❏ ❏ #8: Flashpoint
❏ ❏ #9: The Big Dig
❏ ❏ #10: Deep Pockets
❏ ❏ #11: Heart of the World
❏ ❏ #12: Lie Down With the Devil
❏ ❏ # _____

BARR, NEVADA

Anna Pigeon: While working as a National Park
Ranger, Pigeon investigates murders.

❏ ❏ #1: Track of the Cat
❏ ❏ #2: A Superior Death
❏ ❏ #3: Ill Wind
❏ ❏ #4: Firestorm
❏ ❏ #5: Endangered Species
❏ ❏ #6: Blind Descent
❏ ❏ #7: Liberty Falling
❏ ❏ #8: Deep South
❏ ❏ #9: Blood Lure
❏ ❏ #10: Hunting Season
❏ ❏ #11: Flashback
❏ ❏ #12: High Country
❏ ❏ #13: Hard Truth
❏ ❏ #14: Winter Study
❏ ❏ #15: Borderline
❏ ❏ # _____

BARRETT, LORNA

Tricia Miles: In a town of independent bookstores, people keep getting murdered. Good thing mystery bookstore owner Miles is there.

- ❏ ❏   #1: Murder Is Binding
- ❏ ❏   #2: Bookmarked for Death
- ❏ ❏   #3: Bookplate Special
- ❏ ❏   # _____

BARRON, STEPHANIE

Jane Austen: In between writing her masterpieces, Austen spends her time figuring out mysteries.

- ❏ ❏   #1: Jane and the Unpleasantness at Scargrave Manor
- ❏ ❏   #2: Jane and the Man of the Cloth
- ❏ ❏   #3: Jane and the Wandering Eye
- ❏ ❏   #4: Jane and the Genius of the Place
- ❏ ❏   #5: Jane and the Stillroom Maid
- ❏ ❏   #6: Jane and the Prisoner of Wool House
- ❏ ❏   #7: Jane and the Ghosts of Netley
- ❏ ❏   #8: Jane and His Lordship's Legacy
- ❏ ❏   #9: Jane and the Barque of Frailty
- ❏ ❏   # _____

BATTLES, BRETT

Jonathan Quinn: Quinn works as a professional cleaner, disposing of bodies and erasing all evidence of crimes.

- ❏ ❏   #1: The Cleaner
- ❏ ❏   #2: The Deceived
- ❏ ❏   #3: Shadow of Betrayal
- ❏ ❏   # _____

Beaton, M.C.

Agatha Raisin: Raisin is a retired public-relations-agent-turned-private-detective in the English Midlands.

- ❑ ❑ #1: Agatha Raisin and the Quiche of Death
- ❑ ❑ #2: Agatha Raisin and the Vicious Vet
- ❑ ❑ #3: Agatha Raisin and the Potted Gardener
- ❑ ❑ #4: Agatha Raisin and the Walkers of Dembley
- ❑ ❑ #5: Agatha Raisin and the Murderous Marriage
- ❑ ❑ #6: Agatha Raisin and the Terrible Tourist
- ❑ ❑ #7: Agatha Raisin and the Wellspring of Death
- ❑ ❑ #8: Agatha Raisin and the Wizard of Evesham
- ❑ ❑ #9: Agatha Raisin and the Witch of Wyckhadden
- ❑ ❑ #10: Agatha Raisin and the Fairies of Fryfam
- ❑ ❑ #11: Agatha Raisin and the Love from Hell
- ❑ ❑ #12: Agatha Raisin and the Day the Floods Came
- ❑ ❑ #13: Agatha Raisin and the Case of the Curious Curate
- ❑ ❑ #14: Agatha Raisin and the Haunted House
- ❑ ❑ #15: The Deadly Dance
- ❑ ❑ #16: Agatha Raisin and the Perfect Paragon
- ❑ ❑ #17: Love, Lies and Liquor
- ❑ ❑ #18: Kissing Christmas Goodbye
- ❑ ❑ #19: Agatha Raisin and a Spoonful of Poison
- ❑ ❑ #20: There Goes the Bride
- ❑ ❑ # _____

Hamish MacBeth: Macbeth is a police officer in the colorful town of Lochdubh, Scotland.

- ❑ ❑ #1: Death of a Gossip
- ❑ ❑ #2: Death of a Cad
- ❑ ❑ #3: Death of an Outsider
- ❑ ❑ #4: Death of a Perfect Wife
- ❑ ❑ #5: Death of a Hussy
- ❑ ❑ #6: Death of a Snob

❏	❏	#7: Death of a Prankster
❏	❏	#8: Death of a Glutton
❏	❏	#9: Death of a Travelling Man
❏	❏	#10: Death of a Charming Man
❏	❏	#11: Death of a Nag
❏	❏	#12: Death of a Macho Man
❏	❏	#13: Death of a Dentist
❏	❏	#14: Death of a Scriptwriter
❏	❏	#15: Death of an Addict
❏	❏	#16: A Highland Christmas
❏	❏	#17: Death of a Dustman
❏	❏	#18: Death of a Celebrity
❏	❏	#19: Death of a Village
❏	❏	#20: Death of a Poison Pen
❏	❏	#21: Death of a Bore
❏	❏	#22: Death of a Dreamer
❏	❏	#23: Death of a Maid
❏	❏	#24: Death of a Gentle Lady
❏	❏	#25: Death of a Witch
❏	❏	# _____

BEBRIS, CARRIE A.

Mr. And Mrs. Darcy: Newlyweds Elizabeth Bennet and Mr. Darcy from Pride and Prejudice solve mysteries that correlate with other Austen novels.

❏	❏	#1: Pride and Prescience
❏	❏	#2: Suspense and Sensibility
❏	❏	#3: North by Northanger
❏	❏	#4: The Matters at Mansfield
❏	❏	# _____

BENN, JAMES R.

Billy Boyle: Lt. Boyle is an American officer in Europe in the 1940s. He cracks war-related crimes while dealing with the moral implications of World War II.

- ❏ ❏ #1: Billy Boyle
- ❏ ❏ #2: The First Wave
- ❏ ❏ #3: Blood Alone
- ❏ ❏ #4: Evil for Evil
- ❏ ❏ # _____

BERNHARDT, WILLIAM

Ben Kincaid: Kincaid is a young lawyer trying to find justice in the system. (Good luck with that!)

- ❏ ❏ #1: Primary Justice
- ❏ ❏ #2: Blind Justice
- ❏ ❏ #3: Deadly Justice
- ❏ ❏ #4: Perfect Justice
- ❏ ❏ #5: Cruel Justice
- ❏ ❏ #6: Naked Justice
- ❏ ❏ #7: Extreme Justice
- ❏ ❏ #8: Dark Justice
- ❏ ❏ #9: Silent Justice
- ❏ ❏ #10: Murder One
- ❏ ❏ #11: Criminal Intent
- ❏ ❏ #12: Death Row
- ❏ ❏ #13: Hate Crime
- ❏ ❏ #14: Capitol Murder
- ❏ ❏ #15: Capitol Threat
- ❏ ❏ #16: Capitol Conspiracy
- ❏ ❏ #17: Capitol Offense
- ❏ ❏ # _____

BILLHEIMER, JOHN

Owen Allison: Allison is a civil engineer who often specializes in failure analysis. The problem with that job is that so much of the failure is from foul play.

- ❏ ❏ #1: The Contrary Blues
- ❏ ❏ #2: Highway Robbery
- ❏ ❏ #3: Dismal Mountain
- ❏ ❏ #4: Drybone Hollow
- ❏ ❏ #5: Stonewall Jackson's Elbow
- ❏ ❏ # _____

BLACK, CARA

Aimée Léduc: Léduc is a private investigator who unravels crimes in and around Paris with the help of her dwarf partner René Friant.

- ❏ ❏ #1: Murder in the Marais
- ❏ ❏ #2: Murder in Belleville
- ❏ ❏ #3: Murder in the Sentier
- ❏ ❏ #4: Murder in the Bastille
- ❏ ❏ #5: Murder in Clichy
- ❏ ❏ #6: Murder in Montmartre
- ❏ ❏ #7: Murder on the Ile Saint-Louis
- ❏ ❏ #8: Murder in the Rue de Paradis
- ❏ ❏ #9: Murder in the Latin Quarter
- ❏ ❏ # _____

BLACK, MICHAEL A.

Ron Shade: Private detective Shade doesn't always have all the answers to his personal life, but he's darn good about figuring out mysteries in Chicago.

- ❏ ❏ #1: A Killing Frost
- ❏ ❏ #2: Windy City Knights
- ❏ ❏ #3: A Final Judgment

❏ ❏ #4: Dead Ringer (with Julie Hyzy)
❏ ❏ # _____

Bliss, Miranda

Cooking Class Mysteries: Annie and Eve are best
friends who decide to broaden their horizons by taking
cooking classes.
❏ ❏ #1: Cooking Up Murder
❏ ❏ #2: Murder on the Menu
❏ ❏ #3: Dead Men Don't Get the Munchies
❏ ❏ #4: Dying for Dinner
❏ ❏ #5: Murder Has a Sweet Tooth
❏ ❏ # _____

Block, Lawrence

Bernie Rhodenbarr: Rhodenbarr is a "gentleman
burglar" who often stumbles onto murders.
❏ ❏ #1: Burglars Can't Be Choosers
❏ ❏ #2: The Burglar in the Closet
❏ ❏ #3: The Burglar Who Liked to Quote Kipling
❏ ❏ #4: The Burglar Who Studied Spinoza
❏ ❏ #5: The Burglar Who Painted Like Mondrian
❏ ❏ #6: The Burglar Who Traded Ted Williams
❏ ❏ #7: The Burglar Who Thought He Was Bogart
❏ ❏ #8: The Burglar in the Library
❏ ❏ #9: The Burglar in the Rye
❏ ❏ #10: The Burglar on the Prowl
❏ ❏ # _____

Keller: Keller is a lonely hitman for hire who often
travels around to different cities for his clients.
❏ ❏ #1: Hit Man
❏ ❏ #2: Hit List

❏ ❏ #3: Hit Parade
❏ ❏ #4: Hit and Run
❏ ❏ # _____

Matthew Scudder: Scudder struggles with alcoholism while working as an unlicensed private investigator.

❏ ❏ #1: In the Midst of Death
❏ ❏ #2: The Sins of the Fathers
❏ ❏ #3: Time to Murder and Create
❏ ❏ #4: A Stab in the Dark
❏ ❏ #5: Eight Million Ways to Die
❏ ❏ #6: When the Sacred Ginmill Closes
❏ ❏ #7: Out on the Cutting Edge
❏ ❏ #8: A Ticket to the Boneyard
❏ ❏ #9: A Dance at the Slaughterhouse
❏ ❏ #10: A Walk Among the Tombstones
❏ ❏ #11: The Devil Knows You're Dead
❏ ❏ #12: A Long Line of Dead Men
❏ ❏ #13: Even the Wicked
❏ ❏ #14: Everybody Dies
❏ ❏ #15: Hope to Die
❏ ❏ #16: All the Flowers Are Dying
❏ ❏ # _____

BLUNT, GILES

John Cardinal: Equipped with a mysterious past and a loner mentality, Cardinal serves as a homicide detective in the small Canadian town of Algonquin Bay.

❏ ❏ #1: Forty Words for Sorrow
❏ ❏ #2: The Delicate Storm
❏ ❏ #3: Black Fly Season
❏ ❏ #4: By the Time You Read This
❏ ❏ # _____

BOOTH, STEPHEN

Cooper and Fry: Police detectives Ben Cooper and
Diane Fry solve grisly murders in the Peak District.

❏ ❏ #1: Black Dog
❏ ❏ #2: Dancing With the Virgins
❏ ❏ #3: Blood on the Tongue
❏ ❏ #4: Blind to the Bones
❏ ❏ #5: One Last Breath
❏ ❏ #6: The Dead Place
❏ ❏ #7: Scared to Live
❏ ❏ #8: Dying to Sin
❏ ❏ # _____

BOWEN, MICHAEL

Rep and Melissa Pennyworth: Rep is a lawyer and
Melissa is a professor.

❏ ❏ #1: Screen Scam
❏ ❏ #2: Unforced Error
❏ ❏ #3: Putting Lipstick on a Pig
❏ ❏ #4: Shoot the Lawyer Twice
❏ ❏ #5: Service Dress Blues
❏ ❏ # _____

BOWEN, RHYS

Evan Evans: Constable Evans is a police officer in the
village of Llanfair, which is located in Wales. Despite
his silly name, he manages to crack all sorts of crimes.

❏ ❏ #1: Evans Above
❏ ❏ #2: Evan Help Us
❏ ❏ #3: Evanly Choirs
❏ ❏ #4: Evan and Elle
❏ ❏ #5: Evan Can Wait
❏ ❏ #6: Evans to Betsy

❑ ❑ #7: Evan Only Knows
❑ ❑ #8: Evan's Gate
❑ ❑ #9: Evan Blessed
❑ ❑ #10: Evanly Bodies
❑ ❑ # _____

Her Royal Spyness: Lady Victoria Georgiana Charlotte Eugenie has been asked to be a spy for the Queen in 1930s London.
❑ ❑ #1: Her Royal Spyness
❑ ❑ #2: A Royal Pain
❑ ❑ #3: Royal Flush
❑ ❑ # _____

Molly Murphy: Murphy is an Irish immigrant living in New York during the early 20th century.
❑ ❑ #1: Murphy's Law
❑ ❑ #2: Death of Riley
❑ ❑ #3: For the Love of Mike
❑ ❑ #4: In Like Flynn
❑ ❑ #5: Oh Danny Boy
❑ ❑ #6: In Dublin's Fair City
❑ ❑ #7: Tell Me, Pretty Maiden
❑ ❑ #8: In a Gilded Cage
❑ ❑ # _____

Box, C.J.

Joe Pickett: Pickett is a game warden and family man in Wyoming.
❑ ❑ #1: Open Season
❑ ❑ #2: Savage Run
❑ ❑ #3: Winterkill
❑ ❑ #4: Trophy Hunt
❑ ❑ #5: Out of Range

❏ ❏ #6: In Plain Sight
❏ ❏ #7: Free Fire
❏ ❏ #8: Blood Trail
❏ ❏ #9: Below Zero
❏ ❏ # _____

Brandreth, Gyles

Oscar Wilde: In addition to being a playwright, poet and author, Oscar Wilde also solved mysteries. That's a true story, except for the truth part.

❏ ❏ #1: Oscar Wilde and a Death of No Importance
❏ ❏ #2: Oscar Wilde and a Game Called Murder
❏ ❏ #3: Oscar Wilde and the Dead Man's Smile
❏ ❏ # _____

Braun, Lilian Jackson

Cat Who…: Reporter James Qwilleran and his two Siamese cats, Koko and Yum-Yum, tackle an unprecedented number of crimes.

❏ ❏ #1: The Cat Who Could Read Backwards
❏ ❏ #2: The Cat Who Ate Danish Modern
❏ ❏ #3: The Cat Who Turned On and Off
❏ ❏ #4: The Cat Who Saw Red
❏ ❏ #5: The Cat Who Played Brahms
❏ ❏ #6: The Cat Who Played Post Office
❏ ❏ #7: The Cat Who Knew Shakespeare
❏ ❏ #8: The Cat Who Sniffed Glue
❏ ❏ #9: The Cat Who Went Underground
❏ ❏ #10: The Cat Who Talked to Ghosts
❏ ❏ #11: The Cat Who Lived High
❏ ❏ #12: The Cat Who Knew a Cardinal
❏ ❏ #13: The Cat Who Moved a Mountain
❏ ❏ #14: The Cat Who Wasn't There
❏ ❏ #15: The Cat Who Went Into the Closet

❏ ❏ #16: The Cat Who Came to Breakfast
❏ ❏ #17: The Cat Who Blew the Whistle
❏ ❏ #18: The Cat Who Said Cheese
❏ ❏ #19: The Cat Who Tailed a Thief
❏ ❏ #20: The Cat Who Sang for the Birds
❏ ❏ #21: The Cat Who Saw Stars
❏ ❏ #22: The Cat Who Robbed a Bank
❏ ❏ #23: The Cat Who Smelled a Rat
❏ ❏ #24: The Cat Who Went Up the Creek
❏ ❏ #25: The Cat Who Brought Down the House
❏ ❏ #26: The Cat Who Talked Turkey
❏ ❏ #27: The Cat Who Went Bananas
❏ ❏ #28: The Cat Who Dropped a Bombshell
❏ ❏ #29: The Cat Who Had 60 Whiskers
❏ ❏ # _____

BROGAN, JAN

Hallie Ahern: Ahern solves cases by reporting the stories for a newspaper in Rhode Island.
❏ ❏ #1: Confidential Source
❏ ❏ #2: Yesterday's Fatal
❏ ❏ #3: Teaser
❏ ❏ # _____

BROWN, DAN

Robert Langton: Langton unveils conspiracies by connecting improbable series of clues in historic locations.
❏ ❏ #1: Angels & Demons
❏ ❏ #2: The Da Vinci Code
❏ ❏ #3: The Lost Symbol
❏ ❏ # _____

Brown, Rita Mae

Jane Arnold: Arnold is the master of the Jefferson Hunt Club in Virginia.

❏ ❏ #1: Outfoxed
❏ ❏ #2: Hotspur
❏ ❏ #3: Full Cry
❏ ❏ #4: Hunt Ball
❏ ❏ #5: The Hounds and the Fury
❏ ❏ #6: The Tell-Tale Horse
❏ ❏ #7: Hounded to Death
❏ ❏ # _____

Mrs. Murphy: Justice League, Crozet, Virginia style: Mary Minor "Harry" Haristeen (Human), Mrs. Murphy (Cat), Pewter (Cat) and Tee Tucker (Dog).

❏ ❏ #1: Wish You Were Here
❏ ❏ #2: Rest in Pieces
❏ ❏ #3: Murder at Monticello
❏ ❏ #4: Pay Dirt
❏ ❏ #5: Murder, She Meowed
❏ ❏ #6: Murder on the Prowl
❏ ❏ #7: Cat on the Scent
❏ ❏ #8: Pawing Through the Past
❏ ❏ #9: Claws and Effect
❏ ❏ #10: Catch as Cat Can
❏ ❏ #11: The Tail of the Tip-Off
❏ ❏ #12: Whisker of Evil
❏ ❏ #13: Cat's Eyewitness
❏ ❏ #14: Sour Puss
❏ ❏ #15: Puss 'n Cahoots
❏ ❏ #16: The Purrfect Murder
❏ ❏ #17: Santa Clawed
❏ ❏ # _____

BRUEN, KEN

Inspector Brant: Brant serves as a Detective Sergeant
for the Metropolitan police in London.
- ❏ ❏ #1: A White Arrest
- ❏ ❏ #2: Taming the Alien
- ❏ ❏ #3: The McDead
- ❏ ❏ #4: Blitz
- ❏ ❏ #5: Vixen
- ❏ ❏ #6: Calibre
- ❏ ❏ #7: Ammunition
- ❏ ❏ # _____

Jack Taylor: Taylor is a disgraced ex-cop in Galway
who seems to be spiraling downward into alcoholism
and despair
- ❏ ❏ #1: The Guards
- ❏ ❏ #2: The Killing of the Tinkers
- ❏ ❏ #3: The Magdalen Martyrs
- ❏ ❏ #4: The Dramatist
- ❏ ❏ #5: Priest
- ❏ ❏ #6: Cross
- ❏ ❏ #7: Sanctuary
- ❏ ❏ # _____

BRUNS, DON

Caribbean: Mick Sever has an awesome job as a rock
and roll journalist, but it isn't as much fun when people
get murdered.
- ❏ ❏ #1: Jamaica Blue
- ❏ ❏ #2: Barbados Heat
- ❏ ❏ #3: South Beach Shakedown
- ❏ ❏ #4: St. Barts Breakdown
- ❏ ❏ # _____

Stuff: James Lessor and Skip Moore bought a white box truck to start a hauling business.

- ❏ ❏ #1: Stuff to Die For
- ❏ ❏ #2: Stuff Dreams Are Made Of
- ❏ ❏ #3: Stuff to Spy For
- ❏ ❏ # _____

BUCKLEY, FIONA

Ursula Blanchard: Blanchard works for Queen Elizabeth I, solving murders and unraveling conspiracies.

- ❏ ❏ #1: To Shield the Queen
- ❏ ❏ #2: The Doublet Affair
- ❏ ❏ #3: Queen's Ransom
- ❏ ❏ #4: To Ruin a Queen
- ❏ ❏ #5: Queen of Ambition
- ❏ ❏ #6: A Pawn for a Queen
- ❏ ❏ #7: The Fugitive Queen
- ❏ ❏ #8: The Siren Queen
- ❏ ❏ # _____

BURKE, JAMES LEE

Billy Bob Holland: Holland used to be a cop and Texas Ranger, but now works as an attorney.

- ❏ ❏ #1: Cimarron Rose
- ❏ ❏ #2: Heartwood
- ❏ ❏ #3: Bitterroot
- ❏ ❏ #4: In the Moon of Red Ponies
- ❏ ❏ # _____

Dave Robicheaux: Robicheaux is a former New Orleans police officer turned detective in New Iberia, LA.

- ❏ ❏ #1: The Neon Rain

- ❏ ❏ #2: Heaven's Prisoners
- ❏ ❏ #3: Black Cherry Blues
- ❏ ❏ #4: A Morning for Flamingos
- ❏ ❏ #5: A Stained White Radiance
- ❏ ❏ #6: In the Electric Mist with Confederate Dead
- ❏ ❏ #7: Dixie City Jam
- ❏ ❏ #8: Burning Angel
- ❏ ❏ #9: Cadillac Jukebox
- ❏ ❏ #10: Sunset Limited
- ❏ ❏ #11: Purple Cane Road
- ❏ ❏ #12: Jolie Blon's Bounce
- ❏ ❏ #13: Last Car to Elysian Fields
- ❏ ❏ #14: Crusader's Cross
- ❏ ❏ #15: Pegasus Descending
- ❏ ❏ #16: The Tin Roof Blowdown
- ❏ ❏ #17: Swan Peak
- ❏ ❏ # _____

BURKE, JAN

Irene Kelly: Newspaperwoman Kelly catches the dangerous and tough stories in southern California.
- ❏ ❏ #1: Goodnight, Irene
- ❏ ❏ #2: Sweet Dreams, Irene
- ❏ ❏ #3: Dear Irene
- ❏ ❏ #4: Remember Me, Irene
- ❏ ❏ #5: Hocus
- ❏ ❏ #6: Liar
- ❏ ❏ #7: Bones
- ❏ ❏ #8: Flight
- ❏ ❏ #9: Bloodlines
- ❏ ❏ #10: Kidnapped
- ❏ ❏ # _____

Butcher, Jim

The Dresden Files: Harry Dresden is a wizard and a private detective in Chicago.

❑ ❑ #1: Storm Front
❑ ❑ #2: Fool Moon
❑ ❑ #3: Grave Peril
❑ ❑ #4: Summer Knight
❑ ❑ #5: Death Masks
❑ ❑ #6: Blood Rites
❑ ❑ #7: Dead Beat
❑ ❑ #8: Proven Guilty
❑ ❑ #9: White Night
❑ ❑ #10: Small Favor
❑ ❑ #11: Turn Coat
❑ ❑ # _____

Cameron, Dana

Emma Fielding: Archaeologist Fielding has a nice job at a respectable university in New England.

❑ ❑ #1: Grave Consequences
❑ ❑ #2: Site Unseen
❑ ❑ #3: Past Malice
❑ ❑ #4: A Fugitive Truth
❑ ❑ #5: More Bitter Than Death
❑ ❑ #6: Ashes and Bones
❑ ❑ # _____

Cannell, Dorothy

Ellie Haskell: Haskell is an interior decorator who works with a plucky sidekick, Mrs. Malloy.

❑ ❑ #1: The Thin Woman
❑ ❑ #2: Down the Garden Path
❑ ❑ #3: The Widows Club

❏ ❏ #4: Mum's the Word
❏ ❏ #5: Femmes Fatal
❏ ❏ #6: How to Murder Your Mother-in-Law
❏ ❏ #7: How to Murder the Man of Your Dreams
❏ ❏ #8: The Spring Cleaning Murders
❏ ❏ #9: The Trouble with Harriet
❏ ❏ #10: Bridesmaids Revisited
❏ ❏ #11: The Importance of Being Ernestine
❏ ❏ #13: Goodbye, Ms. Chips
❏ ❏ #14: She Shoots to Conquer
❏ ❏ # _____

CARL, JOANNA

Chocoholic Mysteries: In the resort town of Warner
Pier, Michigan, Lee McKinney manages the family
chocolate business.
❏ ❏ #1: The Chocolate Cat Caper
❏ ❏ #2: The Chocolate Bear Burglary
❏ ❏ #3: The Chocolate Frog Frame-Up
❏ ❏ #4: The Chocolate Puppy Puzzle
❏ ❏ #5: The Chocolate Mouse Trap
❏ ❏ #6: The Chocolate Bridal Bash
❏ ❏ #7: The Chocolate Jewel Case
❏ ❏ #8: The Chocolate Snowman Murders
❏ ❏ #9: The Chocolate Cupid Killings
❏ ❏ # _____

CARTER, SAMMI

Candy Shop: Abby Shaw runs a candy shop in Paradise,
Colorado.
❏ ❏ #1: Candy Apple Dead
❏ ❏ #2: Chocolate-Dipped Death
❏ ❏ #3: Peppermint Twisted

❏ ❏ #4: Goody Goody Gunshots
❏ ❏ #5: Sucker Punch
❏ ❏ # _____

CHERCOVER, SEAN

Ray Dudgeon: Dudgeon was a newspaper reporter, but now he is a Chicago-based private detective.
❏ ❏ #1: Big City, Bad Blood
❏ ❏ #2: Trigger City
❏ ❏ # _____

CHILD, LEE

Jack Reacher: Reacher is an ex-military policeman who now is a drifter who wanders around the country getting into trouble.
❏ ❏ #1: Killing Floor
❏ ❏ #2: Die Trying
❏ ❏ #3: Tripwire
❏ ❏ #4: Running Blind
❏ ❏ #5: Echo Burning
❏ ❏ #6: Without Fail
❏ ❏ #7: Persuader
❏ ❏ #8: The Enemy
❏ ❏ #9: One Shot
❏ ❏ #10: The Hard Way
❏ ❏ #11: Bad Luck and Trouble
❏ ❏ #12: Nothing to Lose
❏ ❏ #13: Gone Tomorrow
❏ ❏ # _____

CHILDS, LAURA

Scrapbooking: Carmela Bertrand runs the New Orleans Memory Mine, a scrapbooking shop.

- ❏ ❏ #1: Keepsake Crimes
- ❏ ❏ #2: Photo Finished
- ❏ ❏ #3: Bound for Murder
- ❏ ❏ #4: Motif for Murder
- ❏ ❏ #5: Frill Kill
- ❏ ❏ #6: Death Swatch
- ❏ ❏ #7: Tragic Magic
- ❏ ❏ # _____

Tea Shop: Theodosia Browning owns Charleston's Indigo Tea Shop.

- ❏ ❏ #1: Death by Darjeeling
- ❏ ❏ #2: Gunpowder Green
- ❏ ❏ #3: Shades of Earl Grey
- ❏ ❏ #4: The English Breakfast Murder
- ❏ ❏ #5: The Jasmine Moon Murder
- ❏ ❏ #6: Chamomile Mourning
- ❏ ❏ #7: Blood Orange Brewing
- ❏ ❏ #8: Dragonwell Dead
- ❏ ❏ #9: The Silver Needle Murder
- ❏ ❏ #10: Oolong Dead
- ❏ ❏ # _____

CLARE, ALYS

Hawkenlye: In Hawkenlye, Abbess Helewise manages a community of nuns and monks during the reign of Richard the Lionheart.

- ❏ ❏ #1: Fortune Like the Moon
- ❏ ❏ #2: Ashes of the Elements
- ❏ ❏ #3: The Tavern in the Morning
- ❏ ❏ #4: The Chatter of the Maidens

❏ ❏ #5: The Faithful Dead
❏ ❏ #6: A Dark Night Hidden
❏ ❏ #7: Whiter Than the Lily
❏ ❏ #8: Girl in a Red Tunic
❏ ❏ #9: Heart of Ice
❏ ❏ #10: The Enchanter's Forest
❏ ❏ #11: The Paths of the Air
❏ ❏ #12: Joys of My Life
❏ ❏ # _____

CLARK, CAROL HIGGINS

Regan Reilly: Miami Beach PI Reilly is the daughter of a mystery writer.

❏ ❏ #1: Decked
❏ ❏ #2: Snagged
❏ ❏ #3: Iced
❏ ❏ #4: Twanged
❏ ❏ #5: Fleeced
❏ ❏ #6: Jinxed
❏ ❏ #7: Popped
❏ ❏ #8: Burned
❏ ❏ #9: Hitched
❏ ❏ #10: Laced
❏ ❏ #11: Zapped
❏ ❏ #12: Cursed
❏ ❏ # _____

CLELAND, JANE K.

Josie Prescott: Antiques appraiser Prescott left New York after being a whistle blower at an auction house. Now she runs her own business in New Hampshire.

❏ ❏ #1: Consigned To Death
❏ ❏ #2: Deadly Appraisal

❑ ❑ #3: Antiques To Die For
❑ ❑ #4: Killer Keepsakes
❑ ❑ # _____

CLEMENS, JUDY

Stella Crown: Crown is a dairy woman by day and a biker by night. When does she solve mysteries? All the time.

❑ ❑ #1: Till the Cows Come Home
❑ ❑ #2: Three Can Keep a Secret
❑ ❑ #3: To Thine Own Self Be True
❑ ❑ #4: The Day Will Come
❑ ❑ #5: Different Paths
❑ ❑ # _____

CLEMENT, BLAIZE

Dixie Hemingway: Hemingway is a pet-sitter in Sarasota, FL.

❑ ❑ #1: Curiosity Killed the Cat Sitter
❑ ❑ #2: Duplicity Dogged the Dachshund
❑ ❑ #3: Even Cat Sitters Get the Blues
❑ ❑ #4: Cat Sitter on a Hot Tin Roof
❑ ❑ # _____

CLEVERLY, BARBARA

Joe Sandilands: Sandilands is a World War I hero who now serves as a Scotland Yard detective, initially in India before returning to England.

❑ ❑ #1: The Last Kashmiri Rose
❑ ❑ #2: Ragtime in Simla
❑ ❑ #3: The Damascened Blade
❑ ❑ #4: The Palace Tiger

❑ ❑ #5: The Bee's Kiss
❑ ❑ #6: Tug of War
❑ ❑ #7: Folly Du Jour
❑ ❑ # _____

Laetitia Talbot: Talbot is an archaeologist working in Europe during the 1920s.
❑ ❑ #1: The Tomb of Zeus
❑ ❑ #2: Bright Hair About the Bone
❑ ❑ # _____

COBEN, HARLAN

Myron Bolitar: Sports agent Bolitar deals with his clients' problems with the help of his morally questionable sidekick Win.
❑ ❑ #1: Deal Breaker
❑ ❑ #2: Drop Shot
❑ ❑ #3: Fade Away
❑ ❑ #4: Back Spin
❑ ❑ #5: One False Move
❑ ❑ #6: The Final Detail
❑ ❑ #7: Darkest Fear
❑ ❑ #8: Promise Me
❑ ❑ #9: Long Lost
❑ ❑ # _____

COEL, MARGARET

John O'Malley & Vicky Holden: Father O'Malley is a pastor of St. Francis Mission and Holden is a lawyer for the Arapaho. Together they investigate murders on Wyoming's Wind River Reservation.
❑ ❑ #1: The Eagle Catcher
❑ ❑ #2: The Ghost Walker

❏ ❏ #3: The Dream Stalker
❏ ❏ #4: The Story Teller
❏ ❏ #5: The Lost Bird
❏ ❏ #6: The Spirit Woman
❏ ❏ #7: The Thunder Keeper
❏ ❏ #8: The Shadow Dancers
❏ ❏ #9: Killing Raven
❏ ❏ #10: Wife of Moon
❏ ❏ #11: Eye of the Wolf
❏ ❏ #12: The Drowning Man
❏ ❏ #13: The Girl with Braided Hair
❏ ❏ #14: The Silent Spirit
❏ ❏ # _____

COGGINS, MARK

August Riordan: PI Riordan is also a jazz bass player when he's not working on cases that sometimes involve technology.

❏ ❏ #1: The Immortal Game
❏ ❏ #2: Vulture Capital
❏ ❏ #3: Candy from Strangers
❏ ❏ #4: Runoff
❏ ❏ #5: The Big Wake Up
❏ ❏ # _____

COHEN, JEFFREY

Double Feature: Elliot Freed runs a movie theatre in New Jersey that specializes in comedy.

❏ ❏ #1: Some Like It Hot-Buttered
❏ ❏ #2: It Happened One Knife
❏ ❏ #3: A Night at the Operation
❏ ❏ # _____

COLBERT, CURT

Jake Rossiter: In 1940s Seattle, WWII veteran Rossiter solves murders with his lovely sidekick Miss Jenkins.

❑ ❑ #1: Rat City
❑ ❑ #2: Sayonaraville
❑ ❑ #3: Queer Street
❑ ❑ # _____

COLEMAN, REED FARREL

Moe Prager: In the 1970s, Prager is a private detective haunted by the destructive secrets he keeps.

❑ ❑ #1: Walking the Perfect Square
❑ ❑ #2: Redemption Street
❑ ❑ #3: The James Deans
❑ ❑ #4: Soul Patch
❑ ❑ #5: Empty Ever After
❑ ❑ # _____

COLLINS, KATE

Flower Shop: Abby Knight dropped out of law school and now runs a flower shop.

❑ ❑ #1: Mum's the Word
❑ ❑ #2: Slay It with Flowers
❑ ❑ #3: Dearly Depotted
❑ ❑ #4: Snipped in the Bud
❑ ❑ #5: Acts of Violets
❑ ❑ #6: A Rose from the Dead
❑ ❑ #7: Shoots to Kill
❑ ❑ #8: Evil in Carnations
❑ ❑ # _____

COLLINS, MAX ALLAN

Quarry: Quarry is a no-nonsense killer for hire.
- ❏ ❏ #1: Quarry
- ❏ ❏ #2: Quarry's Deal
- ❏ ❏ #3: Quarry's List
- ❏ ❏ #4: Quarry's Cut
- ❏ ❏ #5: Primary Target
- ❏ ❏ #6: The Last Quarry
- ❏ ❏ #7: The First Quarry
- ❏ ❏ #8: Quarry in the Middle
- ❏ ❏ # _____

CONNELLY, MICHAEL

Harry Bosch: Former Vietnam tunnel rat turned LAPD detective, Bosch peers into the darkness without falling in.
- ❏ ❏ #1: The Black Echo
- ❏ ❏ #2: The Black Ice
- ❏ ❏ #3: The Concrete Blonde
- ❏ ❏ #4: The Last Coyote
- ❏ ❏ #5: Trunk Music
- ❏ ❏ #6: Angels Flight
- ❏ ❏ #7: A Darkness More Than Night
- ❏ ❏ #8: City of Bones
- ❏ ❏ #9: Lost Light
- ❏ ❏ #10: The Narrows
- ❏ ❏ #11: The Closers
- ❏ ❏ #12: Echo Park
- ❏ ❏ #13: The Overlook
- ❏ ❏ #14: The Brass Verdict
- ❏ ❏ #15: Nine Dragons
- ❏ ❏ # _____

Mickey Heller: LA attorney Heller drives a Lincoln and defends those who may or may not be guilty.

❏ ❏ #1: The Lincoln Lawyer
❏ ❏ #2: The Brass Verdict
❏ ❏ # _____

CORNWELL, PATRICIA

Kay Scarpetta: Scarpetta now has a private forensic pathology practice and tackles some of the grittiest cases.

❏ ❏ #1: Postmortem
❏ ❏ #2: Body of Evidence
❏ ❏ #3: All That Remains
❏ ❏ #4: Cruel and Unusual
❏ ❏ #5: The Body Farm
❏ ❏ #6: From Potter's Field
❏ ❏ #7: Cause of Death
❏ ❏ #8: Unnatural Exposure
❏ ❏ #9: Point of Origin
❏ ❏ #10: Black Notice
❏ ❏ #11: The Last Precinct
❏ ❏ #12: Blow Fly
❏ ❏ #13: Trace
❏ ❏ #14: Predator
❏ ❏ #15: Book of the Dead
❏ ❏ #16: Scarpetta
❏ ❏ # _____

COTTERILL, COLIN

Dr. Siri Paiboun: Dr. Siri is the state coroner for the Lao People's Democratic Republic in the 1970s. He got the job because he's practically the only doctor left in Laos.

❏ ❏ #1: The Coroner's Lunch
❏ ❏ #2: Thirty-Three Teeth

❏ ❏ #3: Disco for the Departed
❏ ❏ #4: Anarchy and Old Dogs
❏ ❏ #5: Curse of the Pogo Stick
❏ ❏ #6: The Merry Misogynist
❏ ❏ # _____

COYLE, CLEO

Coffeehouse Mysteries: Clare Cosi runs a coffeehouse in New York's Greenwich Village.
❏ ❏ #1: On What Grounds
❏ ❏ #2: Through the Grinder
❏ ❏ #3: Latte Trouble
❏ ❏ #4: Murder Most Frothy
❏ ❏ #5: Decaffeinated Corpse
❏ ❏ #6: French Pressed
❏ ❏ #7: Espresso Shot
❏ ❏ #8: Holiday Grind
❏ ❏ # _____

CRAIS, ROBERT

Elvis Cole: Cole is in many ways the classic LA private investigator. His sidekick Joe Pike is formidable.
❏ ❏ #1: The Monkey's Raincoat
❏ ❏ #2: Stalking the Angel
❏ ❏ #3: Lullaby Town
❏ ❏ #4: Free Fall
❏ ❏ #5: Voodoo River
❏ ❏ #6: Sunset Express
❏ ❏ #7: Indigo Slam
❏ ❏ #8: LA Requiem
❏ ❏ #9: The Last Detective
❏ ❏ #10: The Forgotten Man
❏ ❏ #11: Chasing Darkness
❏ ❏ # _____

CROMBIE, DEBORAH

Duncan Kincaid: Kincaid and Gemma James are Scotland Yard detectives who are personally and professionally entwined.

- ❏ ❏ #1: A Share in Death
- ❏ ❏ #2: All Shall Be Well
- ❏ ❏ #3: Leave the Grave Green
- ❏ ❏ #4: Mourn Not Your Dead
- ❏ ❏ #5: Dreaming of the Bones
- ❏ ❏ #6: Kissed a Sad Goodbye
- ❏ ❏ #7: A Finer End
- ❏ ❏ #8: And Justice There Is None
- ❏ ❏ #9: Now May You Weep
- ❏ ❏ #10: In a Dark House
- ❏ ❏ #11: Water Like a Stone
- ❏ ❏ #12: Where Memories Lie
- ❏ ❏ #13: Necessary as Blood
- ❏ ❏ # _____

DAHEIM, MARY

Judith McMonigle Flynn: Flynn's Hillside Manor Inn is a very cozy bed-and-breakfast, aside from the unusual number of deaths.

- ❏ ❏ #1: Just Desserts
- ❏ ❏ #2: Fowl Prey
- ❏ ❏ #3: Holy Terrors
- ❏ ❏ #4: Dune to Death
- ❏ ❏ #5: Bantam of the Opera
- ❏ ❏ #6: A Fit of Tempera
- ❏ ❏ #7: Major Vices
- ❏ ❏ #8: Murder, My Suite
- ❏ ❏ #9: Auntie Mayhem
- ❏ ❏ #10: Nutty as a Fruitcake
- ❏ ❏ #11: September Mourn

- ❏ ❏ #12: Wed and Buried
- ❏ ❏ #13: Snow Place to Die
- ❏ ❏ #14: Legs Benedict
- ❏ ❏ #15: Creeps Suzette
- ❏ ❏ #16: A Streetcar Named Expire
- ❏ ❏ #17: Suture Self
- ❏ ❏ #18: Silver Scream
- ❏ ❏ #19: Hocus Croakus
- ❏ ❏ #20: This Old Souse
- ❏ ❏ #21: Dead Man Docking
- ❏ ❏ #22: Saks and Violins
- ❏ ❏ #23: Scots on the Rocks
- ❏ ❏ #24: Vi Agra Falls
- ❏ ❏ # _____

Emma Lord: In Washington's Cascade Mountains, Lord serves as the publisher-editor of The Alpine Advocate.
- ❏ ❏ #1: The Alpine Advocate
- ❏ ❏ #2: The Alpine Betrayal
- ❏ ❏ #3: The Alpine Christmas
- ❏ ❏ #4: The Alpine Decoy
- ❏ ❏ #5: The Alpine Escape
- ❏ ❏ #6: The Alpine Fury
- ❏ ❏ #7: The Alpine Gamble
- ❏ ❏ #8: The Alpine Hero
- ❏ ❏ #9: The Alpine Icon
- ❏ ❏ #10: The Alpine Journey
- ❏ ❏ #11: The Alpine Kindred
- ❏ ❏ #12: The Alpine Legacy
- ❏ ❏ #13: The Alpine Menace
- ❏ ❏ #14: The Alpine Nemesis
- ❏ ❏ #15: The Alpine Obituary
- ❏ ❏ #16: The Alpine Pursuit
- ❏ ❏ #17: The Alpine Quilt

- ❏ ❏ #18: The Alpine Recluse
- ❏ ❏ #19: The Alpine Scandal
- ❏ ❏ #20: The Alpine Traitor
- ❏ ❏ #21: The Alpine Uproar
- ❏ ❏ # _____

D'Amato, Barbara

Cat Marsala: Marsala is a freelance journalist in Chicago who tackles the hard cases.
- ❏ ❏ #1: Hardball
- ❏ ❏ #2: Hard Tack
- ❏ ❏ #3: Hard Luck
- ❏ ❏ #4: Hard Women
- ❏ ❏ #5: Hard Case
- ❏ ❏ #6: Hard Christmas
- ❏ ❏ #7: Hard Bargain
- ❏ ❏ #8: Hard Evidence
- ❏ ❏ #9: Hard Road
- ❏ ❏ # _____

Dams, Jeanne M.

Dorothy Martin: Martin is a Hoosier native who moves to England after her husband's death.
- ❏ ❏ #1: The Body in the Transept
- ❏ ❏ #2: Trouble in the Town Hall
- ❏ ❏ #3: Holy Terror in the Hebrides
- ❏ ❏ #4: Malice in Miniature
- ❏ ❏ #5: The Victim in Victoria Station
- ❏ ❏ #6: Killing Cassidy
- ❏ ❏ #7: To Perish in Penzance
- ❏ ❏ #8: Sins Out of School
- ❏ ❏ #9: Winter of Discontent
- ❏ ❏ # _____

Hilda Johansson: Johansson is a housemaid to the very
wealthy Studebaker family in the early 1900s.
- ❏ ❏ #1: Death in Lacquer Red
- ❏ ❏ #2: Red, White, and Blue Murder
- ❏ ❏ #3: Green Grow the Victims
- ❏ ❏ #4: Silence Is Golden
- ❏ ❏ #5: Crimson Snow
- ❏ ❏ #6: Indigo Christmas
- ❏ ❏ # _____

DAMSGAARD, SHIRLEY

Ophelia and Abby: Ophelia Jenson lives with her
grandmother Abby. She discovers that she has psychic
powers and that Abby is a witch.
- ❏ ❏ #1: Witch Way to Murder
- ❏ ❏ #2: Charmed to Death
- ❏ ❏ #3: The Trouble with Witches
- ❏ ❏ #4: Witch Hunt
- ❏ ❏ #5: The Witch Is Dead
- ❏ ❏ #6: The Witch's Grave
- ❏ ❏ # _____

DANIELS, CASEY

Pepper Martin: After hitting her head on Gus Scarpetti's
mausoleum, Martin can see dead people. They want her
help.
- ❏ ❏ #1: Don of the Dead
- ❏ ❏ #2: The Chick and the Dead
- ❏ ❏ #3: Tombs of Endearment
- ❏ ❏ #4: Night of the Loving Dead
- ❏ ❏ #5: Dead Man Talking
- ❏ ❏ # _____

Davidson, Diane Mott

Goldy Schultz: Schulz is a caterer in Colorado whose recipes are to die for.

❏ ❏ #1: Catering to Nobody
❏ ❏ #2: Dying for Chocolate
❏ ❏ #3: The Cereal Murders
❏ ❏ #4: The Last Suppers
❏ ❏ #5: Killer Pancake
❏ ❏ #6: The Main Corpse
❏ ❏ #7: The Grilling Season
❏ ❏ #8: Prime Cut
❏ ❏ #9: Tough Cookie
❏ ❏ #10: Sticks & Scones
❏ ❏ #11: Chopping Spree
❏ ❏ #12: Double Shot
❏ ❏ #13: Dark Tort
❏ ❏ #14: Sweet Revenge
❏ ❏ #15: Fatally Flaky
❏ ❏ #_____

Davis, Kyra

Sophie Katz: Katz is a half-black, half-Jewish mystery author who also gets to the bottom of real crimes with the help of sexy PI Anatoly Darinsky.

❏ ❏ #1: Sex, Murder and a Double Latte
❏ ❏ #2: Passion, Betrayal and Killer Highlights
❏ ❏ #3: Obsession, Deceit and Really Dark Chocolate
❏ ❏ #4: Lust, Loathing and a Little Lip Gloss
❏ ❏ #_____

DAVIS, LINDSEY

Marcus Didius Falco: Falco is a private investigator, amateur poet and family man in 70 AD Rome.

- ❑ ❑ #1: The Silver Pigs
- ❑ ❑ #2: Shadows in Bronze
- ❑ ❑ #3: Venus in Copper
- ❑ ❑ #4: The Iron Hand of Mars
- ❑ ❑ #5: Poseidon's Gold
- ❑ ❑ #6: Last Act in Palmyra
- ❑ ❑ #7: Time to Depart
- ❑ ❑ #8: A Dying Light in Corduba
- ❑ ❑ #9: Three Hands in the Fountain
- ❑ ❑ #10: Two For the Lions
- ❑ ❑ #11: One Virgin Too Many
- ❑ ❑ #12: Ode to a Banker
- ❑ ❑ #13: A Body in the Bathhouse
- ❑ ❑ #14: The Jupiter Myth
- ❑ ❑ #15: The Accusers
- ❑ ❑ #16: Scandal Takes a Holiday
- ❑ ❑ #17: See Delphi and Die
- ❑ ❑ #18: Saturnalia
- ❑ ❑ #19: Alexandria
- ❑ ❑ # _____

DEAVER, JEFFERY

Kathryn Dance: Dance is a California interrogation expert who specializes in the scientific evaluation of hidden clues in body language.

- ❑ ❑ #1: The Sleeping Doll
- ❑ ❑ #2: Roadside Crosses
- ❑ ❑ # _____

Lincoln Rhyme: Rhyme was the head of NYPD forensics, but after an accident he is a quadriplegic who can move only one finger.

❏ ❏ #1: The Bone Collector
❏ ❏ #2: The Coffin Dancer
❏ ❏ #3: The Empty Chair
❏ ❏ #4: The Stone Monkey
❏ ❏ #5: The Vanished Man
❏ ❏ #6: The Twelfth Card
❏ ❏ #7: The Cold Moon
❏ ❏ #8: The Broken Window
❏ ❏ # _____

DERESKE, JO

Helma Zukas: Librarian extraordinaire Zukas solves crimes with her avant-garde artist friend Ruth Winthrop.

❏ ❏ #1: Miss Zukas and the Library Murders
❏ ❏ #2: Miss Zukas and the Island Murders
❏ ❏ #3: Miss Zukas and the Stroke of Death
❏ ❏ #4: Miss Zukas and the Raven's Dance
❏ ❏ #5: Out of Circulation
❏ ❏ #6: Final Notice
❏ ❏ #7: Miss Zukas in Death's Shadow
❏ ❏ #8: Miss Zukas Shelves the Evidence
❏ ❏ #9: Bookmarked to Die
❏ ❏ #10: Catalogue of Death
❏ ❏ #11: Index to Murder
❏ ❏ # _____

DICKINSON, DAVID

Lord Francis Powerscourt: Irish investigator
Powerscourt solves murders at the turn of the 20th
century.

- ❏ ❏ #1: Goodnight Sweet Prince
- ❏ ❏ #2: Death and the Jubilee
- ❏ ❏ #3: Death of an Old Master
- ❏ ❏ #4: Death of a Chancellor
- ❏ ❏ #5: Death Called to the Bar
- ❏ ❏ #6: Death On the Nevskii Prospekt
- ❏ ❏ #7: Death on the Holy Mountain
- ❏ ❏ #8: Death of a Pilgrim
- ❏ ❏ # _____

DISHER, GARRY

Inspector Challis: Challis and his team crack murders in
Australia.

- ❏ ❏ #1: The Dragon Man
- ❏ ❏ #2: Kittyhawk Down
- ❏ ❏ #3: Snapshot
- ❏ ❏ #4: Chain of Evidence
- ❏ ❏ #5: Blood Moon
- ❏ ❏ # _____

DODSON, BRANDT

Colton Parker: Parker is a single parent and a private
detective working in Indianapolis, where he also
struggles with his faith.

- ❏ ❏ #1: Original Sin
- ❏ ❏ #2: Seventy Times Seven
- ❏ ❏ #3: The Root of All Evil
- ❏ ❏ #4: The Lost Sheep
- ❏ ❏ # _____

DORSEY, TIM

Serge A. Storms: Storms is a homicidal psychopath who goes around Florida with madcap results.

- ❏ ❏ #1: Florida Roadkill
- ❏ ❏ #2: Hammerhead Ranch Motel
- ❏ ❏ #3: Orange Crush
- ❏ ❏ #4: Triggerfish Twist
- ❏ ❏ #5: Stingray Shuffle
- ❏ ❏ #6: Cadillac Beach
- ❏ ❏ #7: Torpedo Juice
- ❏ ❏ #8: Big Bamboo
- ❏ ❏ #9: Hurricane Punch
- ❏ ❏ #10: Atomic Lobster
- ❏ ❏ #11: Nuclear Jellyfish
- ❏ ❏ # _____

DOSS, JAMES D.

Charlie Moon: Among the Utes of Colorado, Moon is a tribal policeman who works with a shaman named Aunt Daisy.

- ❏ ❏ #1: The Shaman Sings
- ❏ ❏ #2: The Shaman Laughs
- ❏ ❏ #3: The Shaman's Bones
- ❏ ❏ #4: The Shaman's Game
- ❏ ❏ #5: The Night Visitor
- ❏ ❏ #6: Grandmother Spider
- ❏ ❏ #7: White Shell Woman
- ❏ ❏ #8: Dead Soul
- ❏ ❏ #9: The Witch's Tongue
- ❏ ❏ #10: Shadow Man
- ❏ ❏ #11: Stone Butterfly
- ❏ ❏ #12: Three Sisters
- ❏ ❏ #13: Snake Dreams

❏ ❏ #14: The Widow's Revenge

❏ ❏ # _____

DOUGLAS, CAROLE NELSON

Midnight Louie: Louie is an overweight black cat who solves mysteries along with his owner, Temple Barr, a freelance public relations consultant.

❏ ❏ #1: Catnap

❏ ❏ #2: Pussyfoot

❏ ❏ #3: Cat on a Blue Monday

❏ ❏ #4: Cat in a Crimson Haze

❏ ❏ #5: Cat in a Diamond Dazzle

❏ ❏ #6: Cat with an Emerald Eye

❏ ❏ #7: Cat in a Flamingo Fedora

❏ ❏ #8: Cat in a Golden Garland

❏ ❏ #9: Cat on a Hyacinth Hunt

❏ ❏ #10: Cat in an Indigo Mood

❏ ❏ #11: Cat in a Jeweled Jumpsuit

❏ ❏ #12: Cat in a Kiwi Con

❏ ❏ #13: Cat in a Leopard Spot

❏ ❏ #14: Cat in a Midnight Choir

❏ ❏ #15: Cat in a Neon Nightmare

❏ ❏ #16: Cat in an Orange Twist

❏ ❏ #17: Cat in a Hot Pink Pursuit

❏ ❏ #18: Cat in a Quicksilver Caper

❏ ❏ #19: Cat in a Red Hot Rage

❏ ❏ #20: Cat in a Sapphire Slipper

❏ ❏ #21: Cat in a Topaz Tango

❏ ❏ # _____

DOWNIE, RUTH

Gaius Petreius Ruso: Ruso is a Roman Army medic and reluctant sleuth in the year 118 AD.

❏ ❏ #1: Medicus

❏ ❏   #2: Terra Incognita
❏ ❏   #3: Persona Non Grata
❏ ❏   # _____

Driver, Lee

Chase Dagger: Dagger is a private detective who's also an amnesiac. He works with a shapeshifter on some odd cases.

❏ ❏   #1: The Good Die Twice
❏ ❏   #2: Full Moon, Bloody Moon
❏ ❏   #3: The Unseen
❏ ❏   #4: Chasing Ghosts
❏ ❏   # _____

Dunlap, Phil

Piedmont Kelly: US Marshal Kelly covers the violent Southwest, resolving mysteries in the Arizona Territories in the 1880s.

❏ ❏   #1: The Death of Desert Belle
❏ ❏   #2: Fatal Revenge
❏ ❏   #3: Blood on the Rimrock
❏ ❏   # _____

Dunn, Carola

Daisy Dalrymple: In 1920s England, Dalrymple takes up writing for Town & Country magazine.

❏ ❏   #1: Death at Wentwater Court
❏ ❏   #2: The Winter Garden Mystery
❏ ❏   #3: Requiem for a Mezzo
❏ ❏   #4: Murder on the Flying Scotsman
❏ ❏   #5: Damsel in Distress
❏ ❏   #6: Dead in the Water
❏ ❏   #7: Styx and Stones

❏ ❏ #8: Rattle His Bones
❏ ❏ #9: To Davy Jones Below
❏ ❏ #10: The Case of the Murdered Muckraker
❏ ❏ #11: Mistletoe and Murder
❏ ❏ #12: Die Laughing
❏ ❏ #13: A Mourning Wedding
❏ ❏ #14: Fall of a Philanderer
❏ ❏ #15: Gunpowder Plot
❏ ❏ #16: The Bloody Tower
❏ ❏ #17: Black Ship
❏ ❏ #18: Sheer Folly
❏ ❏ # _____

DUNNING, JOHN

Cliff Janeway: Burnt-out cop Janeway trades in his badge to work as a bookseller.
❏ ❏ #1: Booked to Die
❏ ❏ #2: The Bookman's Wake
❏ ❏ #3: The Bookman's Promise
❏ ❏ #4: The Sign of the Book
❏ ❏ #5: The Bookwoman's Last Fling
❏ ❏ # _____

EDWARDS, RUTH DUDLEY

Robert Amiss: Trouble follows Amiss through a variety of jobs in England.
❏ ❏ #1: Corridors of Death
❏ ❏ #2: The Saint Valentine's Day Murders
❏ ❏ #3: The English School of Murder
❏ ❏ #4: Clubbed to Death
❏ ❏ #5: Matricide at St. Martha's
❏ ❏ #6: Ten Lords A-Leaping
❏ ❏ #7: Murder in a Cathedral
❏ ❏ #8: Publish and Be Murdered

- ❏ ❏ #9: The Anglo-Irish Murders
- ❏ ❏ #10: Carnage on the Committee
- ❏ ❏ #11: Murdering Americans
- ❏ ❏ # _____

EHRMAN, KIT

Steve Cline: Cline works as a barn manager, tending to horses.

- ❏ ❏ #1: At Risk
- ❏ ❏ #2: Dead Man's Touch
- ❏ ❏ #3: Cold Burn
- ❏ ❏ #4: Triple Cross
- ❏ ❏ # _____

EISLER, BARRY

John Rain: Rain is a half-Japanese, half-American assassin based in Tokyo.

- ❏ ❏ #1: Rain Fall
- ❏ ❏ #2: Hard Rain
- ❏ ❏ #3: Rain Storm
- ❏ ❏ #4: Killing Rain
- ❏ ❏ #5: The Last Assassin
- ❏ ❏ #6: Requiem for an Assassin
- ❏ ❏ # _____

ELKINS, AARON

Gideon Oliver: Forensic anthropologist Oliver is known as the "bone detective."

- ❏ ❏ #1: Fellowship of Fear
- ❏ ❏ #2: The Dark Place
- ❏ ❏ #3: Murder in the Queen's Armes
- ❏ ❏ #4: Old Bones
- ❏ ❏ #5: Curses!

❏ ❏ #6: Icy Clutches
❏ ❏ #7: Make No Bones
❏ ❏ #8: Dead Men's Hearts
❏ ❏ #9: Twenty Blue Devils
❏ ❏ #10: Skeleton Dance
❏ ❏ #11: Good Blood
❏ ❏ #12: Where There's a Will
❏ ❏ #13: Unnatural Selection
❏ ❏ #14: Little Tiny Teeth
❏ ❏ #15: Uneasy Relations
❏ ❏ # _____

ELLIS, KATE

Wesley Peterson: Detective Sergeant Peterson is also an amateur archaeologist.

❏ ❏ #1: The Merchant's House
❏ ❏ #2: The Armada Boy
❏ ❏ #3: An Unhallowed Grave
❏ ❏ #4: The Funeral Boat
❏ ❏ #5: The Bone Garden
❏ ❏ #6: A Painted Doom
❏ ❏ #7: The Skeleton Room
❏ ❏ #8: The Plague Maiden
❏ ❏ #9: A Cursed Inheritance
❏ ❏ #10: The Marriage Hearse
❏ ❏ #11: The Shining Skull
❏ ❏ # _____

EMERSON, KATHY LYNN

Susanna, Lady Appleton: Lady Appleton is a 16th century gentlewoman and herbalist.

❏ ❏ #1: Face Down in the Marrow-Bone Pie
❏ ❏ #2: Face Down Upon an Herbal
❏ ❏ #3: Face Down Among the Winchester Geese

❏ ❏ #4: Face Down Beneath the Eleanor Cross
❏ ❏ #5: Face Down Under the Wych Elm
❏ ❏ #6: Face Down Before the Rebel Hooves
❏ ❏ #7: Face Down Across the Western Sea
❏ ❏ #8: Face Down Below the Banqueting House
❏ ❏ #9: Face Down Beside St. Anne's Well
❏ ❏ #10: Face Down O'er the Border
❏ ❏ # _____

Estleman, Loren D.

Amos Walker: Walker is a private detective in Detroit.
❏ ❏ #1: Motor City Blue
❏ ❏ #2: Angel Eyes
❏ ❏ #3: The Midnight Man
❏ ❏ #4: The Glass Highway
❏ ❏ #5: Sugartown
❏ ❏ #6: Every Brilliant Eye
❏ ❏ #7: Lady Yesterday
❏ ❏ #8: Downriver
❏ ❏ #9: General Murders
❏ ❏ #10: Silent Thunder
❏ ❏ #11: Sweet Women Lie
❏ ❏ #12: Never Street
❏ ❏ #13: The Witchfinder
❏ ❏ #14: The Hours of the Virgin
❏ ❏ #15: A Smile on the Face of the Tiger
❏ ❏ #16: Sinister Heights
❏ ❏ #17: Poison Blonde
❏ ❏ #18: Retro
❏ ❏ #19: Nicotine Kiss
❏ ❏ #20: American Detective
❏ ❏ # _____

Valentino: Valentino works as a film detective for UCLA, searching for old lost prints of films.

❏ ❏ #1: Frames
❏ ❏ #2: Alone
❏ ❏ # _____

EVANOVICH, JANET

Stephanie Plum: Plum is a Jersey bounty hunter who gets entangled in comical crimes in numerical order.

❏ ❏ #1: One for the Money
❏ ❏ #2: Two for the Dough
❏ ❏ #3: Three to Get Deadly
❏ ❏ #4: Four to Score
❏ ❏ #5: High Five
❏ ❏ #6: Hot Six
❏ ❏ #7: Seven Up
❏ ❏ #8: Hard Eight
❏ ❏ #9: To the Nines
❏ ❏ #10: Ten Big Ones
❏ ❏ #11: Eleven on Top
❏ ❏ #12: Twelve Sharp
❏ ❏ #13: Lean Mean Thirteen
❏ ❏ #14: Fearless Fourteen
❏ ❏ #15: Finger Lickin' Fifteen
❏ ❏ # _____

EVANS, MARY ANNA

Faye Longchamp: Longchamp is an archaeology graduate student who excavates sites in the Southeast.

❏ ❏ #1: Artifacts
❏ ❏ #2: Relics
❏ ❏ #3: Effigies
❏ ❏ #4: Findings

❏ ❏   #5: Floodgates
❏ ❏   # _____

FAHERTY, TERENCE

Owen Keane: Failed seminarian Keane struggles with life's big questions.
❏ ❏   #1: Deadstick
❏ ❏   #2: Live to Regret
❏ ❏   #3: The Lost Keats
❏ ❏   #4: Die Dreaming
❏ ❏   #5: Prove the Nameless
❏ ❏   #6: The Ordained
❏ ❏   #7: Orion Rising
❏ ❏   # _____

Scott Elliot: Elliott is a private investigator working during the golden age of Hollywood.
❏ ❏   #1: Kill Me Again
❏ ❏   #2: Come Back Dead
❏ ❏   #3: Raise the Devil
❏ ❏   #4: In a Teapot
❏ ❏   # _____

FERRIS, MONICA

Needlecraft: Betsy Devonshire untangles murders that revolve around her needlecraft store in Excelsior, Minnesota.
❏ ❏   #1: Crewel World
❏ ❏   #2: Framed in Lace
❏ ❏   #3: A Stitch in Time
❏ ❏   #4: Unraveled Sleeve
❏ ❏   #5: A Murderous Yarn
❏ ❏   #6: Hanging by a Thread

❏ ❏ #7: Cutwork
❏ ❏ #8: Crewel Yule
❏ ❏ #9: Embroidered Truths
❏ ❏ #10: Sins and Needles
❏ ❏ #11: Knitting Bones
❏ ❏ #12: Thai Die
❏ ❏ #13: Blackwork
❏ ❏ # _____

FFORDE, JASPER

Thursday Next: Next is a cop in an alternate 1980s England. She is a literary detective who can actually enter books.

❏ ❏ #1: The Eyre Affair
❏ ❏ #2: Lost in a Good Book
❏ ❏ #3: The Well of Lost Plots
❏ ❏ #4: Something Rotten
❏ ❏ #5: Thursday Next: First Among Sequels
❏ ❏ # _____

FIFFER, SHARON

Jane Wheel: Wheel was fired from her PR job and now makes a living in the antiques market.

❏ ❏ #1: Killer Stuff
❏ ❏ #2: Dead Guy's Stuff
❏ ❏ #3: The Wrong Stuff
❏ ❏ #4: Buried Stuff
❏ ❏ #5: Hollywood Stuff
❏ ❏ #6: Scary Stuff
❏ ❏ # _____

Flora, Kate

Thea Kozak: Kozak is a trouble-shooter and consultant for private schools in New England.

- ❏ ❏ #1: Chosen for Death
- ❏ ❏ #2: Death in a Funhouse Mirror
- ❏ ❏ #3: Death at the Wheel
- ❏ ❏ #4: An Educated Death
- ❏ ❏ #5: Death in Paradise
- ❏ ❏ #6: Liberty or Death
- ❏ ❏ #7: Stalking Death
- ❏ ❏ # _____

Fluke, Joanne

Hannah Swensen: Swensen owns a bakery in Lake Eden, Minnesota.

- ❏ ❏ #1: Chocolate Chip Cookie Murder
- ❏ ❏ #2: Strawberry Shortcake Murder
- ❏ ❏ #3: Blueberry Muffin Murder
- ❏ ❏ #4: Lemon Meringue Pie Murder
- ❏ ❏ #5: Fudge Cupcake Murder
- ❏ ❏ #6: Sugar Cookie Murder
- ❏ ❏ #7: Peach Cobbler Murder
- ❏ ❏ #8: Cherry Cheesecake Murder
- ❏ ❏ #9: Key Lime Pie Murder
- ❏ ❏ #10: Carrot Cake Murder
- ❏ ❏ #11: Cream Puff Murder
- ❏ ❏ # _____

Flynn, Vince

Mitch Rapp: Rapp is an American spy who works on the country's most dangerous missions.

- ❏ ❏ #1: Transfer of Power

- ❏ ❏ #2: The Third Option
- ❏ ❏ #3: Separation of Power
- ❏ ❏ #4: Executive Power
- ❏ ❏ #5: Memorial Day
- ❏ ❏ #6: Consent to Kill
- ❏ ❏ #7: Act of Treason
- ❏ ❏ #8: Protect and Defend
- ❏ ❏ #9: Extreme Measures
- ❏ ❏ # _____

FOSSUM, KARIN

Inspector Sejer: Sejer is a no-nonsense policeman who leads a rather sad life in Norway.
- ❏ ❏ #1: Don't Look Back
- ❏ ❏ #2: He Who Fears the Wolf
- ❏ ❏ #3: When the Devil Holds the Candle
- ❏ ❏ #4: The Indian Bride
- ❏ ❏ #5: Black Seconds
- ❏ ❏ #6: The Water's Edge
- ❏ ❏ # _____

FOWLER, CHRISTOPHER

Bryant and May: Arthur Bryant and John May head up the Peculiar Crimes Unit in London.
- ❏ ❏ #1: Full Dark House
- ❏ ❏ #2: The Water Room
- ❏ ❏ #3: Seventy-Seven Clocks
- ❏ ❏ #4: Ten Second Staircase
- ❏ ❏ #5: The White Corridor
- ❏ ❏ #6: The Victoria Vanishes
- ❏ ❏ #7: Bryant & May on the Loose
- ❏ ❏ # _____

FOWLER, EARLENE

Benni Harper: Harper is a curator of a folk art museum and also enjoys quilting.

❑ ❑ #1: Fool's Puzzle
❑ ❑ #2: Irish Chain
❑ ❑ #3: Kansas Troubles
❑ ❑ #4: Goose in the Pond
❑ ❑ #5: Dove in the Window
❑ ❑ #6: Mariner's Compass
❑ ❑ #7: Seven Sisters
❑ ❑ #8: Arkansas Traveler
❑ ❑ #9: Steps to the Altar
❑ ❑ #10: Sunshine and Shadow
❑ ❑ #11: Broken Dishes
❑ ❑ #12: Delectable Mountains
❑ ❑ #13: Tumbling Blocks
❑ ❑ # _____

FRANKLIN, ARIANA

Adelia Aguilar: Aguilar is a medical examiner during the rule of King Henry II.

❑ ❑ #1: Mistress of the Art of Death
❑ ❑ #2: The Serpent's Tale
❑ ❑ #3: Grave Goods
❑ ❑ # _____

FRAZER, MARGARET

Joliffe: During the 1430s, Joliffe is both an actor and a spy.

❑ ❑ #1: A Play of Isaac
❑ ❑ #2: A Play of Dux Moraud
❑ ❑ #3: A Play of Knaves
❑ ❑ #4: A Play of Lords

❏ ❏ #5: A Play of Treachery
❏ ❏ # _____

Sister Frevisse: Frevisse is a nun in England's St.
Frideswide during the 1430s.
❏ ❏ #1: The Novice's Tale
❏ ❏ #2: The Servant's Tale
❏ ❏ #3: The Outlaw's Tale
❏ ❏ #4: The Bishop's Tale
❏ ❏ #5: The Boy's Tale
❏ ❏ #6: The Murderer's Tale
❏ ❏ #7: The Prioress' Tale
❏ ❏ #8: The Maiden's Tale
❏ ❏ #9: The Reeve's Tale
❏ ❏ #10: The Squire's Tale
❏ ❏ #11: The Clerk's Tale
❏ ❏ #12: The Bastard's Tale
❏ ❏ #13: The Hunter's Tale
❏ ❏ #14: The Widow's Tale
❏ ❏ #15: The Sempster's Tale
❏ ❏ #16: The Traitor's Tale
❏ ❏ #17: The Apostate's Tale
❏ ❏ # _____

FREEMAN, BRIAN
Jonathan Stride: Lieutenant Stride is a police officer in
Duluth, Minnesota.
❏ ❏ #1: Immoral
❏ ❏ #2: Stripped
❏ ❏ #3: Stalked
❏ ❏ #4: In the Dark
❏ ❏ # _____

FROMMER, SARA HOSKINSON

Joan Spencer: Spencer is the manager of the Civic
Symphony in Oliver, Indiana.

❏ ❏ #1: Murder in C Major
❏ ❏ #2: Buried in Quilts
❏ ❏ #3: Murder & Sullivan
❏ ❏ #4: The Vanishing Violinist
❏ ❏ #5: Witness in Bishop Hill
❏ ❏ #6: Death Climbs a Tree
❏ ❏ # _____

FULMER, DAVID

Valentin St. Cyr: Creole detective St. Cyr works in New
Orleans at the turn of the 20th century.

❏ ❏ #1: Chasing the Devil's Tail
❏ ❏ #2: Jass
❏ ❏ #3: Rampart Street
❏ ❏ #4: Lost River
❏ ❏ # _____

GAGE, LEIGHTON

Mario Silva: Chief Inspector Silva works for the
Brazilian Federal Police.

❏ ❏ #1: Blood of the Wicked
❏ ❏ #2: Buried Strangers
❏ ❏ #3: Dying Gasp
❏ ❏ # _____

GELLIS, ROBERTA

Magdalene la Batarde: la Batarde is the madam of the
Old Priory Guesthouse in medieval London.

❏ ❏ #1: A Mortal Bane
❏ ❏ #2: A Personal Devil

❑ ❑ #3: Bone of Contention
❑ ❑ #4: Chains of Folly
❑ ❑ # _____

George, Elizabeth

Inspector Lynley: Scotland Yard Inspector Lynley figures out cases with his partner Barbara Havers.

❑ ❑ #1: A Great Deliverance
❑ ❑ #2: Payment in Blood
❑ ❑ #3: Well-Schooled in Murder
❑ ❑ #4: A Suitable Vengeance
❑ ❑ #5: For the Sake of Elena
❑ ❑ #6: Missing Joseph
❑ ❑ #7: Playing for the Ashes
❑ ❑ #8: In the Presence of the Enemy
❑ ❑ #9: Deception on His Mind
❑ ❑ #10: In Pursuit of the Proper Sinner
❑ ❑ #11: A Traitor to Memory
❑ ❑ #12: A Place of Hiding
❑ ❑ #13: With No One as Witness
❑ ❑ #14: What Came Before He Shot Her
❑ ❑ #15: Careless in Red
❑ ❑ # _____

Gerritsen, Tess

Rizzoli/Isles: Homicide detective Jane Rizzoli often uses the help of medical examiner Maura Isles to solve the tough cases in Boston.

❑ ❑ #1: The Surgeon
❑ ❑ #2: The Apprentice
❑ ❑ #3: The Sinner
❑ ❑ #4: Body Double
❑ ❑ #5: Vanish
❑ ❑ #6: The Mephisto Club

❏ ❏ #7: The Keepsake
❏ ❏ # _____

GHELFI, BRENT

Alexei Volkovoy: Volk is a veteran of Russia's war in Chechnya. Now he's a player in the black market and a covert agent for the Russian military.

❏ ❏ #1: Volk's Game
❏ ❏ #2: Volk's Shadow
❏ ❏ #3: The Venona Cable
❏ ❏ # _____

GORDON, ALAN

Fool's Guild: Feste, the fool in Shakespeare's Twelfth Night, is part of a secret CIA-esque Fool's Guild that meddles in affairs throughout 13th century Europe.

❏ ❏ #1: Thirteenth Night
❏ ❏ #2: Jester Leaps In
❏ ❏ #3: A Death in the Venetian Quarter
❏ ❏ #4: The Widow of Jerusalem
❏ ❏ #5: An Antic Disposition
❏ ❏ #6: The Lark's Lament
❏ ❏ #7: The Moneylender of Toulouse
❏ ❏ #8: The Parisian Prodigal
❏ ❏ # _____

GORDON, NADIA

Sunny McCoskey: Napa Valley chef McCoskey looks into the seedier side of the restaurant and wine world when people turn up dead.

❏ ❏ #1: Sharp Shooter
❏ ❏ #2: Death by the Glass
❏ ❏ #3: Murder Alfresco

❏ ❏ #4: Lethal Vintage
❏ ❏ # _____

GRABENSTEIN, CHRIS

John Ceepak: Ceepak is a former military police officer now working for the Sea Haven Police Department on the Jersey Shore. He's partnered with a 24-year-old slacker.

❏ ❏ #1: Tilt a Whirl
❏ ❏ #2: Mad Mouse
❏ ❏ #3: Whack a Mole
❏ ❏ #4: Hell Hole
❏ ❏ #5: Mind Scrambler
❏ ❏ # _____

GRAFTON, SUE

Kinsey Millhone: Millhone is a private investigator who solves cases in alphabetical order in the 1980s.

❏ ❏ #1: A is for Alibi
❏ ❏ #2: B is for Burglar
❏ ❏ #3: C is for Corpse
❏ ❏ #4: D is for Deadbeat
❏ ❏ #5: E is for Evidence
❏ ❏ #6: F is for Fugitive
❏ ❏ #7: G is for Gumshoe
❏ ❏ #8: H is for Homicide
❏ ❏ #9: I is for Innocent
❏ ❏ #10: J is for Judgment
❏ ❏ #11: K is for Killer
❏ ❏ #12: L is for Lawless
❏ ❏ #13: M is for Malice
❏ ❏ #14: N is for Noose
❏ ❏ #15: O is for Outlaw
❏ ❏ #16: P is for Peril

❑ ❑ #17: Q is for Quarry
❑ ❑ #18: R is for Ricochet
❑ ❑ #19: S is for Silence
❑ ❑ #20: T is for Trespass
❑ ❑ #21: U is for Undertow
❑ ❑ # _____

GRAHAM, CAROLINE

Inspector Barnaby: Family man and police officer
Barnaby works cases in the fictional town of Causton,
England.

❑ ❑ #1: The Killings at Badger's Drift
❑ ❑ #2: Death of a Hollow Man
❑ ❑ #3: Death in Disguise
❑ ❑ #4: Written in Blood
❑ ❑ #5: Faithful Unto Death
❑ ❑ #6: A Place of Safety
❑ ❑ #7: A Ghost in the Machine
❑ ❑ # _____

GREENWOOD, KERRY

Corinna Chapman: Chapman is a former
businesswoman turned baker in Melbourne, Australia.

❑ ❑ #1: Earthly Delights
❑ ❑ #2: Heavenly Pleasures
❑ ❑ #3: Devil's Food
❑ ❑ #4: Trick or Treat
❑ ❑ # _____

Phryne Fisher: Fisher is a wealthy aristocrat who also
serves as a detective in 1920s Melbourne.

❑ ❑ #1: Cocaine Blues
❑ ❑ #2: Flying Too High

❏ ❏ #3: Murder on the Ballarat Train
❏ ❏ #4: Death at Victoria Dock
❏ ❏ #5: The Green Mill Murder
❏ ❏ #6: Blood and Circuses
❏ ❏ #7: Ruddy Gore
❏ ❏ #8: Urn Burial
❏ ❏ #9: Raisins and Almonds
❏ ❏ #10: Death Before Wicket
❏ ❏ #11: Away with the Fairies
❏ ❏ #12: Murder in Montparnasse
❏ ❏ #13: The Castlemaine Murders
❏ ❏ #14: Queen of the Flowers
❏ ❏ #15: Death by Water
❏ ❏ #16: Murder in the Dark
❏ ❏ #17: Murder on a Midsummer Night
❏ ❏ # _____

GREGORY, SUSANNA

Matthew Bartholomew: Bartholomew teaches medicine in 14th century Cambridge.
❏ ❏ #1: A Plague on Both Your Houses
❏ ❏ #2: An Unholy Alliance
❏ ❏ #3: A Bone of Contention
❏ ❏ #4: A Deadly Brew
❏ ❏ #5: A Wicked Deed
❏ ❏ #6: A Masterly Murder
❏ ❏ #7: An Order for Death
❏ ❏ #8: A Summer of Discontent
❏ ❏ #9: A Killer in Winter
❏ ❏ #10: The Hand of Justice
❏ ❏ #11: The Mark of a Murderer
❏ ❏ #12: The Tarnished Chalice
❏ ❏ #13: To Kill or Cure
❏ ❏ #14: The Devil's Disciples

❏ ❏ #15: A Vein of Deceit
❏ ❏ # _____

Thomas Chaloner: In Restoration London, Chaloner is a reluctant spy for Secretary of State John Thurloe.
❏ ❏ #1: A Conspiracy of Violence
❏ ❏ #2: Blood on the Strand
❏ ❏ #3: The Butcher of Smithfield
❏ ❏ #4: The Westminster Poisoner
❏ ❏ #5: A Murder on London Bridge
❏ ❏ # _____

GRIMES, MARTHA

Emma Graham: Graham is a twelve-year-old girl who investigates murders at a resort hotel.
❏ ❏ #1: Hotel Paradise
❏ ❏ #2: Cold Flat Junction
❏ ❏ #3: Belle Ruin
❏ ❏ # _____

Richard Jury: Jury is a chief inspector for Scotland Yard. He is usually assisted by aristocrat Melrose Plant and hypochondriac Alfred Wiggins.
❏ ❏ #1: The Man With a Load of Mischief
❏ ❏ #2: The Old Fox Deceiv'd
❏ ❏ #3: The Anodyne Necklace
❏ ❏ #4: The Dirty Duck
❏ ❏ #5: Jerusalem Inn
❏ ❏ #6: The Deer Leap
❏ ❏ #7: Help the Poor Struggler
❏ ❏ #8: I Am the Only Running Footman
❏ ❏ #9: The Five Bells and Bladebone
❏ ❏ #10: The Old Silent
❏ ❏ #11: The Old Contemptibles

❏ ❏ #12: The Horse You Came in On
❏ ❏ #13: Rainbow's End
❏ ❏ #14: The Case has Altered
❏ ❏ #15: The Stargazey
❏ ❏ #16: The Lamorna Wink
❏ ❏ #17: The Blue Last
❏ ❏ #18: The Grave Maurice
❏ ❏ #19: The Winds of Change
❏ ❏ #20: The Old Wine Shades
❏ ❏ #21: Dust
❏ ❏ # _____

GUNN, ELIZABETH

Jake Hines: In Rutherford, Minnesota, Detective Hines deciphers numerical crimes, but starts with the number three just to drive everyone nuts.
❏ ❏ #1: Triple Play
❏ ❏ #2: Par Four
❏ ❏ #3: Five Card Stud
❏ ❏ #4: Six-Pound Walleye
❏ ❏ #5: Seventh-Inning Stretch
❏ ❏ #6: Crazy Eights
❏ ❏ #7: McCafferty's Nine
❏ ❏ #8: The Ten-Mile Trials
❏ ❏ # _____

Sarah Burke: In Tucson, Burke is a detective who works to distract herself from a divorce.
❏ ❏ #1: Cool in Tucson
❏ ❏ #2: New River Blues
❏ ❏ # _____

HADDAM, JANE

Gregor Demarkian: Demarkian is the former head of the FBI's behavioral sciences unit. He is described by one reviewer as an Armenian-American Poirot.

- ❏ ❏ #1: Not a Creature Was Stirring
- ❏ ❏ #2: Precious Blood
- ❏ ❏ #3: Act of Darkness
- ❏ ❏ #4: Quoth the Raven
- ❏ ❏ #5: A Great Day for the Deadly
- ❏ ❏ #6: A Feast of Murder
- ❏ ❏ #7: A Stillness in Bethlehem
- ❏ ❏ #8: Murder Superior
- ❏ ❏ #9: Dear Old Dead
- ❏ ❏ #10: Festival of Deaths
- ❏ ❏ #11: Bleeding Hearts
- ❏ ❏ #12: Fountain of Death
- ❏ ❏ #13: And One to Die On
- ❏ ❏ #14: Baptism in Blood
- ❏ ❏ #15: Deadly Beloved
- ❏ ❏ #16: Skeleton Key
- ❏ ❏ #17: True Believers
- ❏ ❏ #18: Somebody Else's Music
- ❏ ❏ #19: Conspiracy Theory
- ❏ ❏ #20: Headmaster's Wife
- ❏ ❏ #21: Hardscrabble Road
- ❏ ❏ #22: Glass Houses
- ❏ ❏ #23: Cheating at Solitaire
- ❏ ❏ #24: Living Witness
- ❏ ❏ # _____

HAILEY, J.P.

Steve Winslow: As an unconventional lawyer, Winslow wins cases with the help of his assistant, Tracy Garvin.

- ❏ ❏ #1: The Baxter Trust

❑ ❑ #2: The Anonymous Client
❑ ❑ #3: The Underground Man
❑ ❑ #4: The Naked Typist
❑ ❑ #5: The Wrong Gun
❑ ❑ # _____

HAINES, CAROLYN

Southern Belle: Sarah Booth Delaney is a Belle who
lives with a ghost in Mississippi.
❑ ❑ #1: Them Bones
❑ ❑ #2: Buried Bones
❑ ❑ #3: Splintered Bones
❑ ❑ #4: Crossed Bones
❑ ❑ #5: Hallowed Bones
❑ ❑ #6: Bones to Pick
❑ ❑ #7: Ham Bones
❑ ❑ #8: Wishbones
❑ ❑ #9: Greedy Bones
❑ ❑ # _____

HALL, PARNELL

Cora Felton: Felton is the cover girl for the popular
Puzzle Lady crossword franchise.
❑ ❑ #1: A Clue for the Puzzle Lady
❑ ❑ #2: Last Puzzle & Testament
❑ ❑ #3: Puzzled To Death
❑ ❑ #4: A Puzzle in a Pear Tree
❑ ❑ #5: With This Puzzle I Thee Kill
❑ ❑ #6: And a Puzzle to Die On
❑ ❑ #7: Stalking the Puzzle Lady
❑ ❑ #8: You Have the Right to Remain Puzzled
❑ ❑ #9: The Sudoku Puzzle Murders
❑ ❑ #10: Dead Man's Puzzle
❑ ❑ # _____

Stanley Hastings: Hastings is a private detective in New York. He's more cowardly than tough but he still gets the job done.

❏ ❏ #1: Detective
❏ ❏ #2: Murder
❏ ❏ #3: Favor
❏ ❏ #4: Strangler
❏ ❏ #5: Client
❏ ❏ #6: Juror
❏ ❏ #7: Shot
❏ ❏ #8: Actor
❏ ❏ #9: Blackmail
❏ ❏ #10: Movie
❏ ❏ #11: Trial
❏ ❏ #12: Scam
❏ ❏ #13: Suspense
❏ ❏ #14: Cozy
❏ ❏ #15: Manslaughter
❏ ❏ #16: Hitman
❏ ❏ # _____

HALLINAN, TIMOTHY

Poke Rafferty: Rafferty is a travel writer who has settled in Bangkok, where he is trying to build a family.

❏ ❏ #1: A Nail Through the Heart
❏ ❏ #2: The Fourth Watcher
❏ ❏ #3: Breathing Water
❏ ❏ # _____

HAMILTON, STEVE

Alex McKnight: Former Detroit police officer McKnight is haunted by the past as he investigates cases on the Upper Peninsula.

❏ ❏ #1: A Cold Day in Paradise

- ❏ ❏ #2: Winter of the Wolf Moon
- ❏ ❏ #3: The Hunting Wind
- ❏ ❏ #4: North of Nowhere
- ❏ ❏ #5: Blood Is the Sky
- ❏ ❏ #6: Ice Run
- ❏ ❏ #7: A Stolen Season
- ❏ ❏ # _____

HARRIS, C.S.

Sebastian St. Cyr: St. Cyr is asked to help out with investigations in 1810s England.
- ❏ ❏ #1: What Angels Fear
- ❏ ❏ #2: When Gods Die
- ❏ ❏ #3: Why Mermaids Sing
- ❏ ❏ #4: Where Serpents Sleep
- ❏ ❏ #5: What Remains of Heaven
- ❏ ❏ # _____

HARRIS, CHARLAINE

Aurora Teagarden: Teagarden is a librarian and, later, a realtor in Georgia.
- ❏ ❏ #1: Real Murders
- ❏ ❏ #2: A Bone to Pick
- ❏ ❏ #3: Three Bedrooms, One Corpse
- ❏ ❏ #4: The Julius House
- ❏ ❏ #5: Dead Over Heels
- ❏ ❏ #6: A Fool and His Honey
- ❏ ❏ #7: Last Scene Alive
- ❏ ❏ #8: Poppy Done to Death
- ❏ ❏ # _____

Harper Connelly: After being struck by lightening,
Connelly can sense the location and last memories of
the deceased.

- ❏ ❏ #1: Grave Sight
- ❏ ❏ #2: Grave Surprise
- ❏ ❏ #3: An Ice Cold Grave
- ❏ ❏ #4: Grave Secret
- ❏ ❏ # _____

Lily Bard: In Shakespeare, Arkansas, Bard works as a
cleaning lady, and tries to escape her past.

- ❏ ❏ #1: Shakespeare's Landlord
- ❏ ❏ #2: Shakespeare's Champion
- ❏ ❏ #3: Shakespeare's Christmas
- ❏ ❏ #4: Shakespeare's Trollop
- ❏ ❏ #5: Shakespeare's Counselor
- ❏ ❏ # _____

Sookie Stackhouse: This Southern Vampire series is the
basis for the HBO series *True Blood*.

- ❏ ❏ #1: Dead Until Dark
- ❏ ❏ #2: Living Dead in Dallas
- ❏ ❏ #3: Club Dead
- ❏ ❏ #4: Dead to the World
- ❏ ❏ #5: Dead as a Doornail
- ❏ ❏ #6: Definitely Dead
- ❏ ❏ #7: All Together Dead
- ❏ ❏ #8: From Dead to Worse
- ❏ ❏ #9: Dead and Gone
- ❏ ❏ # _____

Harris, Rosemary

Paula Holliday: Holliday was a media executive in the city, but is now a landscape designer in Connecticut.

- ❏ ❏ #1: Pushing Up Daisies
- ❏ ❏ #2: The Big Dirt Nap
- ❏ ❏ # _____

Harrison, Cora

Burren: On the west cost of Ireland in the early 1510s, Mara is the "Brehon of the Burren," a judge.

- ❏ ❏ #1: My Lady Judge
- ❏ ❏ #2: A Secret and Unlawful Killing
- ❏ ❏ #3: The Sting of Justice
- ❏ ❏ #4: Writ in Stone
- ❏ ❏ # _____

Harrod-Eagles, Cynthia

Bill Slider: At the outset of this series, London police detective Slider finds himself drawn to a key witness in a murder case.

- ❏ ❏ #1: Orchestrated Death
- ❏ ❏ #2: Death Watch
- ❏ ❏ #3: Death to Go
- ❏ ❏ #4: Grave Music
- ❏ ❏ #5: Blood Lines
- ❏ ❏ #6: Killing Time
- ❏ ❏ #7: Shallow Grave
- ❏ ❏ #8: Blood Sinister
- ❏ ❏ #9: Gone Tomorrow
- ❏ ❏ #10: Dear Departed
- ❏ ❏ #11: Game Over

❏ ❏   #12: Fell Purpose
❏ ❏   # _____

HART, CAROLYN G.

Bailey Ruth: Traditionalists would say that you have to be alive to investigate mysteries. Ruth, a ghost, would disagree.

❏ ❏   #1: Ghost at Work
❏ ❏   #2: Merry, Merry Ghost
❏ ❏   # _____

Death on Demand: Annie Darling runs the mystery bookstore, Death on Demand, on a resort island community off the coast of South Carolina.

❏ ❏   #1: Death on Demand
❏ ❏   #2: Design for Murder
❏ ❏   #3: Something Wicked
❏ ❏   #4: Honeymoon with Murder
❏ ❏   #5: A Little Class on Murder
❏ ❏   #6: Deadly Valentine
❏ ❏   #7: The Christie Caper
❏ ❏   #8: Southern Ghost
❏ ❏   #9: Mint Julep Murder
❏ ❏   #10: Yankee Doodle Dead
❏ ❏   #11: White Elephant Dead
❏ ❏   #12: Sugarplum Dead
❏ ❏   #13: April Fool Dead
❏ ❏   #14: Engaged to Die
❏ ❏   #15: Murder Walks the Plank
❏ ❏   #16: Death of the Party
❏ ❏   #17: Dead Days of Summer
❏ ❏   #18: Death Walked In
❏ ❏   #19: Dare to Die
❏ ❏   # _____

Henrie O. Collins: Henrie O. has retired from being a newswoman but still comes across stories on her travels.

- ❏ ❏ #1: Dead Man's Island
- ❏ ❏ #2: Scandal in Fair Haven
- ❏ ❏ #3: Death in Lovers' Lane
- ❏ ❏ #4: Death in Paradise
- ❏ ❏ #5: Death on the River Walk
- ❏ ❏ #6: Resort To Murder
- ❏ ❏ #7: Set Sail For Murder
- ❏ ❏ # _____

HART, ELLEN

Jane Lawless: Lawless is a restaurateur in Minneapolis.

- ❏ ❏ #1: Hallowed Murder
- ❏ ❏ #2: Vital Lies
- ❏ ❏ #3: Stage Fright
- ❏ ❏ #4: A Killing Cure
- ❏ ❏ #5: A Small Sacrifice
- ❏ ❏ #6: Faint Praise
- ❏ ❏ #7: Robber's Wine
- ❏ ❏ #8: Wicked Games
- ❏ ❏ #9: Hunting the Witch
- ❏ ❏ #10: The Merchant of Venus
- ❏ ❏ #11: Immaculate Midnight
- ❏ ❏ #12: An Intimate Ghost
- ❏ ❏ #13: The Iron Girl
- ❏ ❏ #14: Night Vision
- ❏ ❏ #15: The Mortal Groove
- ❏ ❏ #16: Sweet Poison
- ❏ ❏ #17: The Mirror and the Mask
- ❏ ❏ # _____

Sophie Greenway: Greenway writes about food in the Twin Cities.

- ❏ ❏ #1: This Little Piggy Went to Murder
- ❏ ❏ #2: For Every Evil
- ❏ ❏ #3: Oldest Sin
- ❏ ❏ #4: Murder in the Air
- ❏ ❏ #5: Slice and Dice
- ❏ ❏ #6: Dial M for Meat Loaf
- ❏ ❏ #7: Death on a Silver Platter
- ❏ ❏ #8: No Reservations Required
- ❏ ❏ # _____

HECHTMAN, BETTY

Crochet: Molly Pink works at a bookstore and belongs to the store's crochet club.

- ❏ ❏ #1: Hooked On Murder
- ❏ ❏ #2: Dead Men Don't Crochet
- ❏ ❏ #3: By Hook or By Crook
- ❏ ❏ # _____

HELLMANN, LIBBY FISCHER

Ellie Foreman: Video documentarian Foreman shoots movies in Chicago.

- ❏ ❏ #1: An Eye for Murder
- ❏ ❏ #2: A Picture of Guilt
- ❏ ❏ #3: An Image of Death
- ❏ ❏ #4: A Shot to Die For
- ❏ ❏ # _____

Georgia Davis: Davis used to be a cop, but now she's a private detective working in Chicago.

- ❏ ❏ #1: Easy Innocence
- ❏ ❏ #2: Doubleback
- ❏ ❏ # _____

HESS, JOAN

Maggody: Arly Hanks is the chief of police in the irregular town of Maggody, Arkansas.

- ❏ ❏ #1: Malice in Maggody
- ❏ ❏ #2: Mischief in Maggody
- ❏ ❏ #3: Much Ado in Maggody
- ❏ ❏ #4: Madness in Maggody
- ❏ ❏ #5: Mortal Remains in Maggody
- ❏ ❏ #6: Maggody in Manhattan
- ❏ ❏ #7: O Little Town of Maggody
- ❏ ❏ #8: Martians in Maggody
- ❏ ❏ #9: Miracles in Maggody
- ❏ ❏ #10: The Maggody Militia
- ❏ ❏ #11: Misery Loves Maggody
- ❏ ❏ #12: Murder@maggody.com
- ❏ ❏ #13: Maggody and the Moonbeams
- ❏ ❏ #14: Muletrain to Maggody
- ❏ ❏ #15: Malpractice in Maggody
- ❏ ❏ # _____

Claire Malloy: Bookstore owner Malloy sells books and clears up mysteries in Faberville, Arkansas.

- ❏ ❏ #1: Strangled Prose
- ❏ ❏ #2: The Murder at the Mimosa Inn
- ❏ ❏ #3: Dear Miss Demeanor
- ❏ ❏ #4: A Really Cute Corpse
- ❏ ❏ #5: A Diet to Die For
- ❏ ❏ #6: Roll Over and Play Dead
- ❏ ❏ #7: Death by the Light of the Moon
- ❏ ❏ #8: Poisoned Pins
- ❏ ❏ #9: Tickled to Death
- ❏ ❏ #10: Busy Bodies
- ❏ ❏ #11: Closely Akin to Murder
- ❏ ❏ #12: A Holly Jolly Murder

- ❏ ❏ #13: A Conventional Corpse
- ❏ ❏ #14: Out on a Limb
- ❏ ❏ #15: The Goodbye Body
- ❏ ❏ #16: Damsels in Distress
- ❏ ❏ #17: Mummy Dearest
- ❏ ❏ # _____

HEWSON, DAVID

Nic Costa: Caravaggio-loving police detective Costa is based in Rome.
- ❏ ❏ #1: A Season for the Dead
- ❏ ❏ #2: The Villa of Mysteries
- ❏ ❏ #3: The Sacred Cut
- ❏ ❏ #4: The Lizard's Bite
- ❏ ❏ #5: The Seventh Sacrament
- ❏ ❏ #6: The Garden of Evil
- ❏ ❏ #7: Dante's Numbers
- ❏ ❏ # _____

HILL, REGINALD

Dalziel & Pascoe: Andrew Dalziel and Peter Pascoe are police detectives in Yorkshire.
- ❏ ❏ #1: A Clubbable Woman
- ❏ ❏ #2: An Advancement of Learning
- ❏ ❏ #3: Ruling Passion
- ❏ ❏ #4: An April Shroud
- ❏ ❏ #5: A Pinch of Snuff
- ❏ ❏ #6: A Killing Kindness
- ❏ ❏ #7: Deadheads
- ❏ ❏ #8: Exit Lines
- ❏ ❏ #9: Child's Play
- ❏ ❏ #10: Under World
- ❏ ❏ #11: Bones and Silence
- ❏ ❏ #12: One Small Step

❑ ❑ #13: Recalled to Life
❑ ❑ #14: Pictures of Perfection
❑ ❑ #15: The Wood Beyond
❑ ❑ #16: Asking for the Moon
❑ ❑ #17: On Beulah Height
❑ ❑ #18: Arms And the Women
❑ ❑ #19: Dialogues of the Dead
❑ ❑ #20: Death's Jest-Book
❑ ❑ #21: Good Morning, Midnight
❑ ❑ #22: Death Comes for the Fat Man
❑ ❑ #23: The Price of Butcher's Meat
❑ ❑ #24: Midnight Fugue
❑ ❑ # _____

Joe Sixsmith: Laid-off lathe operator Sixsmith decides to become a private eye.

❑ ❑ #1: Blood Sympathy
❑ ❑ #2: Born Guilty
❑ ❑ #3: Killing the Lawyers
❑ ❑ #4: Singing the Sadness
❑ ❑ #5: The Roar of the Butterflies
❑ ❑ # _____

HIRAHARA, NAOMI

Mas Arai: Arai is an elderly Japanese American gardener who lives and works in Los Angeles.

❑ ❑ #1: Summer of the Big Bachi
❑ ❑ #2: Gasa-Gasa Girl
❑ ❑ #3: Snakeskin Shamisen
❑ ❑ # _____

HOCKENSMITH, STEVE

Holmes on the Range: Two cowboy brothers are inspired by Sherlock Holmes to travel around the Old West, deducifying everywhere they go.

- ❑ ❑ #1: Holmes on the Range
- ❑ ❑ #2: On the Wrong Track
- ❑ ❑ #3: The Black Dove
- ❑ ❑ #4: The Crack in the Lens
- ❑ ❑ # _____

HOLT, HAZEL

Sheila Malory: Malory is a novelist and a critic working in the English seaside village of Taviscombe.

- ❑ ❑ #1: Mrs. Malory Investigates
- ❑ ❑ #2: The Cruelest Month
- ❑ ❑ #3: Mrs. Malory's Shortest Journey
- ❑ ❑ #4: Mrs. Malory and the Festival Murder
- ❑ ❑ #5: Mrs. Malory: Detective in Residence
- ❑ ❑ #6: Mrs. Malory Wonders Why
- ❑ ❑ #7: Mrs. Malory: Death of a Dean
- ❑ ❑ #8: Mrs. Malory and the Only Good Lawyer
- ❑ ❑ #9: Mrs. Malory: Death Among Friends
- ❑ ❑ #10: Mrs. Malory and the Fatal Legacy
- ❑ ❑ #11: Mrs. Malory and the Lilies That Fester
- ❑ ❑ #12: Mrs. Malory and Death by Water
- ❑ ❑ #13: Mrs. Malory and the Delay of Execution
- ❑ ❑ #14: Mrs. Malory and Death in Practice
- ❑ ❑ #15: Mrs. Malory and the Silent Killer
- ❑ ❑ #16: Mrs. Malory and No Cure for Death
- ❑ ❑ #17: Mrs. Malory and a Death in the Family
- ❑ ❑ #18: Mrs. Malory and a Time To Die
- ❑ ❑ #19: Mrs. Malory and Any Man's Death
- ❑ ❑ # _____

Housewright, David

Holland Taylor: Taylor is a private eye in St. Paul, Minnesota.
- ❏ ❏ #1: Penance
- ❏ ❏ #2: Practice to Deceive
- ❏ ❏ #3: Dearly Departed
- ❏ ❏ # _____

Mac McKenzie: Ex-St. Paul cop McKenzie now spends his time doing favors for friends.
- ❏ ❏ #1: A Hard Ticket Home
- ❏ ❏ #2: Tin City
- ❏ ❏ #3: Pretty Girl Gone
- ❏ ❏ #4: Dead Boyfriends
- ❏ ❏ #5: Madman on a Drum
- ❏ ❏ #6: Jelly's Gold
- ❏ ❏ # _____

Hyzy, Julie

Alex St. James: St. James is a researcher for a television station in Chicago.
- ❏ ❏ #1: Deadly Blessings
- ❏ ❏ #2: Deadly Interest
- ❏ ❏ #3: Dead Ringer (with Michael A. Black)
- ❏ ❏ # _____

Olivia Paras: Paras is Assistant Chef at the White House, responsible for state dinners and a few mysteries too.
- ❏ ❏ #1: State of the Onion
- ❏ ❏ #2: Hail to the Chef
- ❏ ❏ # _____

INDRIDASON, ARNALDUR

Erlendur Sveinsson: In Reykjavik, Detective Inspector Erlendur investigates grisly cases along with his partner Sigurdur Oli.

- ❏ ❏ #1: Jar City
- ❏ ❏ #2: Silence of the Grave
- ❏ ❏ #3: Voices
- ❏ ❏ #4: The Draining Lake
- ❏ ❏ #5: Arctic Chill
- ❏ ❏ # _____

ISLEIB, ROBERTA

Rebecca Butterman: Dr. Butterman is a clinical psychologist who has her own online advice column.

- ❏ ❏ #1: Deadly Advice
- ❏ ❏ #2: Preaching to the Corpse
- ❏ ❏ #3: Asking for Murder
- ❏ ❏ # _____

Cassie Burdette: Burdette is a neurotic professional golfer on the LPGA tour.

- ❏ ❏ #1: Six Strokes Under
- ❏ ❏ #2: A Buried Lie
- ❏ ❏ #3: Putt to Death
- ❏ ❏ #4: Fairway to Heaven
- ❏ ❏ #5: Final Fore
- ❏ ❏ # _____

JAFFARIAN, SUE ANN

Odelia Grey: Grey is a middle-aged, overweight woman who works as a paralegal for a California law firm.

- ❏ ❏ #1: Too Big to Miss
- ❏ ❏ #2: The Curse of the Holy Pail

❑ ❑ #3: Thugs and Kisses
❑ ❑ #4: Booby Trap
❑ ❑ # _____

JAMES, P.D.

Cordelia Gray: Gray inherits a detective agency in London.
❑ ❑ #1: An Unsuitable Job for a Woman
❑ ❑ #2: The Skull Beneath the Skin
❑ ❑ # _____

Adam Dalgliesh: In the Metropolitan Police Service, Commander Dalgliesh is a private person who efficiently settles crimes and dabbles in poetry.
❑ ❑ #1: Cover Her Face
❑ ❑ #2: A Mind to Murder
❑ ❑ #3: Unnatural Causes
❑ ❑ #4: Shroud for a Nightingale
❑ ❑ #5: The Black Tower
❑ ❑ #6: Death of an Expert Witness
❑ ❑ #7: A Taste for Death
❑ ❑ #8: Devices and Desires
❑ ❑ #9: Original Sin
❑ ❑ #10: A Certain Justice
❑ ❑ #11: Death in Holy Orders
❑ ❑ #12: The Murder Room
❑ ❑ #13: The Lighthouse
❑ ❑ #14: The Private Patient
❑ ❑ # _____

JANCE, J.A.

Brandon Walker: A widow experiences trouble with serial killers while surrounded with Native American culture.

- ❏ ❏ #1: Hour of the Hunter
- ❏ ❏ #2: Kiss of the Bees
- ❏ ❏ #3: Day of the Dead
- ❏ ❏ # _____

J.P. Beaumont: Seattle homicide detective Beaumont keeps on solving murders, even after his retirement.

- ❏ ❏ #1: Until Proven Guilty
- ❏ ❏ #2: Injustice for All
- ❏ ❏ #3: Trial by Fury
- ❏ ❏ #4: Taking the Fifth
- ❏ ❏ #5: Improbable Cause
- ❏ ❏ #6: A More Perfect Union
- ❏ ❏ #7: Dismissed with Prejudice
- ❏ ❏ #8: Minor in Possession
- ❏ ❏ #9: Payment in Kind
- ❏ ❏ #10: Without Due Process
- ❏ ❏ #11: Failure to Appear
- ❏ ❏ #12: Lying in Wait
- ❏ ❏ #13: Name Withheld
- ❏ ❏ #14: Breach of Duty
- ❏ ❏ #15: Birds of Prey
- ❏ ❏ #16: Long Time Gone
- ❏ ❏ #17: Justice Denied
- ❏ ❏ #18: Fire and Ice
- ❏ ❏ # _____

Joanna Brady: After her husband is murdered, Brady runs for his position as sheriff of Cochise County, Arizona.

- ❏ ❏ #1: Desert Heat
- ❏ ❏ #2: Tombstone Courage
- ❏ ❏ #3: Shoot, Don't Shoot
- ❏ ❏ #4: Dead to Rights
- ❏ ❏ #5: Skeleton Canyon
- ❏ ❏ #6: Rattlesnake Crossing
- ❏ ❏ #7: Outlaw Mountain
- ❏ ❏ #8: Devil's Claw
- ❏ ❏ #9: Paradise Lost
- ❏ ❏ #10: Partner in Crime
- ❏ ❏ #11: Exit Wounds
- ❏ ❏ #12: Dead Wrong
- ❏ ❏ #13: Damage Control
- ❏ ❏ # _____

JECKS, MICHAEL

Medieval West Country: A former Knight Templar and his friend look into murders.

- ❏ ❏ #1: The Last Templar
- ❏ ❏ #2: The Merchant's Partner
- ❏ ❏ #3: A Moorland Hanging
- ❏ ❏ #4: The Crediton Killings
- ❏ ❏ #5: The Abbot's Gibbet
- ❏ ❏ #6: The Leper's Return
- ❏ ❏ #7: Squire Throwleigh's Heir
- ❏ ❏ #8: Belladonna at Belstone
- ❏ ❏ #9: The Traitor of St. Giles
- ❏ ❏ #10: The Boy-Bishop's Glovemaker
- ❏ ❏ #11: The Tournament of Blood
- ❏ ❏ #12: The Sticklepath Strangler
- ❏ ❏ #13: The Devil's Acolyte

- ❏ ❏ #14: The Mad Monk of Gidleigh
- ❏ ❏ #15: The Templar's Penance
- ❏ ❏ #16: The Outlaws of Ennor
- ❏ ❏ #17: The Tolls of Death
- ❏ ❏ #18: The Chapel of Bones
- ❏ ❏ #19: The Butcher of St. Peters
- ❏ ❏ #20: A Friar's Bloodfeud
- ❏ ❏ #21: The Death Ship of Dartmouth
- ❏ ❏ #22: The Malice of Unnatural Death
- ❏ ❏ #23: Dispensation of Death
- ❏ ❏ #24: The Templar, the Queen and Her Lover
- ❏ ❏ #25: The Prophecy of Death
- ❏ ❏ #26: The King of Thieves
- ❏ ❏ #27: No Law in the Land
- ❏ ❏ # _____

JENNINGS, MAUREEN

William Murdoch: In the 19th century, Detective Murdoch follows crimes throughout Toronto.
- ❏ ❏ #1: Except the Dying
- ❏ ❏ #2: Under the Dragon's Tail
- ❏ ❏ #3: Poor Tom Is Cold
- ❏ ❏ #4: Let Loose the Dogs
- ❏ ❏ #5: Night's Child
- ❏ ❏ #6: Vices of My Blood
- ❏ ❏ #7: A Journeyman to Grief
- ❏ ❏ # _____

JOHANSEN, IRIS

Eve Duncan: Duncan works as a forensic sculptor.
- ❏ ❏ #1: The Face of Deception
- ❏ ❏ #2: The Killing Game
- ❏ ❏ #3: Body of Lies
- ❏ ❏ #4: Blind Alley

❏ ❏ #5: Countdown
❏ ❏ #6: Stalemate
❏ ❏ #7: Quicksand
❏ ❏ #8: Blood Game
❏ ❏ # _____

JOHNSON, CRAIG

Walt Longmire: In Absaroka Country, Wyoming,
Sheriff Longmire investigates crimes with the help of
his friend Henry Standing Bear.
❏ ❏ #1: The Cold Dish
❏ ❏ #2: Death Without Company
❏ ❏ #3: Kindness Goes Unpunished
❏ ❏ #4: Another Man's Moccasins
❏ ❏ #5: The Dark Horse
❏ ❏ # _____

KAMINSKY, STUART M.

Lew Fonesca: Fonesca is as a process server in
Sarasota, Florida.
❏ ❏ #1: Vengeance
❏ ❏ #2: Retribution
❏ ❏ #3: Midnight Pass
❏ ❏ #4: Denial
❏ ❏ #5: Always Say Goodbye
❏ ❏ #6: Bright Futures
❏ ❏ # _____

Abe Lieberman: Lieberman is a Chicago police
sergeant.
❏ ❏ #1: Lieberman's Folly
❏ ❏ #2: Lieberman's Choice
❏ ❏ #3: Lieberman's Day

❏ ❏ #4: Lieberman's Thief
❏ ❏ #5: Lieberman's Law
❏ ❏ #6: The Big Silence
❏ ❏ #7: Not Quite Kosher
❏ ❏ #8: The Last Dark Place
❏ ❏ #9: Terror Town
❏ ❏ #10: The Dead Don't Lie
❏ ❏ # _____

Rostnikov: Inspector Rostnikov is an honest policeman working in post-Soviet Russia.
❏ ❏ #1: Death of a Dissident
❏ ❏ #2: Black Knight in Red Square
❏ ❏ #3: Red Chameleon
❏ ❏ #4: A Cold Red Sunrise
❏ ❏ #5: A Fine Red Rain
❏ ❏ #6: Rostnikov's Vacation
❏ ❏ #7: The Man Who Walked Like a Bear
❏ ❏ #8: Death of a Russian Priest
❏ ❏ #9: Hard Currency
❏ ❏ #10: Blood and Rubles
❏ ❏ #11: Tarnished Icons
❏ ❏ #12: The Dog Who Bit a Policeman
❏ ❏ #13: Fall of a Cosmonaut
❏ ❏ #14: Murder on the Trans-Siberian Express
❏ ❏ #15: People Who Walk in Darkness
❏ ❏ # _____

Toby Peters: PI Peters is hired by the biggest actors and stars during the Golden Age of Hollywood.
❏ ❏ #1: Bullet for a Star
❏ ❏ #2: Murder on the Yellow Brick Road
❏ ❏ #3: You Bet Your Life
❏ ❏ #4: The Howard Hughes Affair

❏ ❏ #5: Never Cross a Vampire
❏ ❏ #6: High Midnight
❏ ❏ #7: Catch a Falling Clown
❏ ❏ #8: He Done Her Wrong
❏ ❏ #9: The Fala Factor
❏ ❏ #10: Down for the Count
❏ ❏ #11: The Man Who Shot Lewis Vance
❏ ❏ #12: Smart Moves
❏ ❏ #13: Think Fast, Mr. Peters
❏ ❏ #14: Buried Caesars
❏ ❏ #15: Poor Butterfly
❏ ❏ #16: The Melting Clock
❏ ❏ #17: The Devil Met a Lady
❏ ❏ #18: Tomorrow Is Another Day
❏ ❏ #19: Dancing in the Dark
❏ ❏ #20: A Fatal Glass of Beer
❏ ❏ #21: A Few Minutes Past Midnight
❏ ❏ #22: To Catch a Spy
❏ ❏ #23: Mildred Pierced
❏ ❏ #24: Now You See It
❏ ❏ # _____

KANDEL, SUSAN

Cece Caruso: Caruso writes biographies of some of the major names in mysteries.

❏ ❏ #1: I Dreamed I Married Perry Mason
❏ ❏ #2: Not a Girl Detective
❏ ❏ #3: Shamus in the Green Room
❏ ❏ #4: Christietown
❏ ❏ #5: Dial H For Hitchcock
❏ ❏ # _____

Kava, Alex

Maggie O'Dell: O'Dell is an FBI Profiler who tracks down some of the worst killers in the country.

- ❏ ❏ #1: A Perfect Evil
- ❏ ❏ #2: Split Second
- ❏ ❏ #3: The Soul Catcher
- ❏ ❏ #4: At the Stroke of Madness
- ❏ ❏ #5: A Necessary Evil
- ❏ ❏ #6: Exposed
- ❏ ❏ #7: Black Friday
- ❏ ❏ # _____

Kellerman, Faye

Peter Decker: Along with his Orthodox Jewish wife Rina Lazarus, Decker investigates murders as an LAPD officer.

- ❏ ❏ #1: The Ritual Bath
- ❏ ❏ #2: Sacred and Profane
- ❏ ❏ #3: Milk and Honey
- ❏ ❏ #4: Day of Atonement
- ❏ ❏ #5: False Prophet
- ❏ ❏ #6: Grievous Sin
- ❏ ❏ #7: Sanctuary
- ❏ ❏ #8: Justice
- ❏ ❏ #9: Prayers for the Dead
- ❏ ❏ #10: Serpent's Tooth
- ❏ ❏ #11: Jupiter's Bones
- ❏ ❏ #12: Stalker
- ❏ ❏ #13: The Forgotten
- ❏ ❏ #14: Stone Kiss
- ❏ ❏ #15: Street Dreams
- ❏ ❏ #16: The Burnt House
- ❏ ❏ #17: The Mercedes Coffin

❏ ❏ #18: Blindman's Bluff
❏ ❏ # _____

Kᴇʟʟᴇʀᴍᴀɴ, Jᴏɴᴀᴛʜᴀɴ

Alex Delaware: Child-psychologist-turned-forensic
psychologist, Delaware consults with police detective
Milo Sturgis on murder cases.
❏ ❏ #1: When the Bough Breaks
❏ ❏ #2: Blood Test
❏ ❏ #3: Over the Edge
❏ ❏ #4: Silent Partner
❏ ❏ #5: Time Bomb
❏ ❏ #6: Private Eyes
❏ ❏ #7: Devil's Waltz
❏ ❏ #8: Bad Love
❏ ❏ #9: Self-Defense
❏ ❏ #10: The Web
❏ ❏ #11: The Clinic
❏ ❏ #12: Survival of the Fittest
❏ ❏ #13: Monster
❏ ❏ #14: Dr. Death
❏ ❏ #15: Flesh and Blood
❏ ❏ #16: The Murder Book
❏ ❏ #17: A Cold Heart
❏ ❏ #18: Therapy
❏ ❏ #19: Rage
❏ ❏ #20: Gone
❏ ❏ #21: Obsession
❏ ❏ #22: Compulsion
❏ ❏ #23: Bones
❏ ❏ #24: Evidence
❏ ❏ # _____

KIMBERLY, ALICE

Haunted Bookshop: Penelope Thornton-McClure runs a bookstore in Rhode Island that is haunted by a ghost who used to be a PI.

❑ ❑ #1: The Ghost and Mrs. McClure
❑ ❑ #2: The Ghost and the Dead Deb
❑ ❑ #3: The Ghost and the Dead Man's Library
❑ ❑ #4: The Ghost and the Femme Fatale
❑ ❑ #5: The Ghost and the Haunted Mansion
❑ ❑ # _____

KING, JONATHON

Max Freeman: After shooting a twelve-year-old child in self defense, Freeman stopped being a cop and relocated to the Everglades.

❑ ❑ #1: The Blue Edge of Midnight
❑ ❑ #2: A Visible Darkness
❑ ❑ #3: Shadow Men
❑ ❑ #4: A Killing Night
❑ ❑ #5: Acts of Nature
❑ ❑ # _____

KING, LAURIE R.

Kate Martinelli: Martinelli is a homicide detective in San Francisco.

❑ ❑ #1: A Grave Talent
❑ ❑ #2: To Play the Fool
❑ ❑ #3: With Child
❑ ❑ #4: Night Work
❑ ❑ #5: The Art of Detection
❑ ❑ # _____

Mary Russell: Sherlock Holmes has retired from the mystery business and is focusing on beekeeping—until he literally stumbles across Russell at age 15.

❏ ❏ #1: The Beekeeper's Apprentice
❏ ❏ #2: A Monstrous Regiment of Women
❏ ❏ #3: A Letter of Mary
❏ ❏ #4: The Moor
❏ ❏ #5: O Jerusalem
❏ ❏ #6: Justice Hall
❏ ❏ #7: The Game
❏ ❏ #8: Locked Rooms
❏ ❏ #9: The Language of Bees
❏ ❏ # _____

KNIGHT, BERNARD

Crowner John: At the end of the 12th century, John de Wolfe works as a coroner in Devon.

❏ ❏ #1: The Sanctuary Seeker
❏ ❏ #2: The Poisoned Chalice
❏ ❏ #3: Crowner's Quest
❏ ❏ #4: The Awful Secret
❏ ❏ #5: The Tinner's Corpse
❏ ❏ #6: The Grim Reaper
❏ ❏ #7: Fear in the Forest
❏ ❏ #8: The Witch Hunter
❏ ❏ #9: Figure of Hate
❏ ❏ #10: The Elixir of Death
❏ ❏ #11: The Noble Outlaw
❏ ❏ #12: The Manor of Death
❏ ❏ #13: Crowner Royal
❏ ❏ # _____

Knopf, Chris

Sam Acquillo: Acquillo is an ex-boxer and an ex-corporate executive who gets involved in misadventures in the Hamptons.

❏ ❏ #1: The Last Refuge
❏ ❏ #2: Two Time
❏ ❏ #3: Head Wounds
❏ ❏ #4: Hard Stop
❏ ❏ # _____

Konrath, J.A.

Jack Daniels: Daniels is a cop working in Chicago, where serial killers attack the city and sometimes those close to her.

❏ ❏ #1: Whiskey Sour
❏ ❏ #2: Bloody Mary
❏ ❏ #3: Rusty Nail
❏ ❏ #4: Dirty Martini
❏ ❏ #5: Fuzzy Navel
❏ ❏ #6: Cherry Bomb
❏ ❏ # _____

Koryta, Michael

Lincoln Perry: Perry is a young PI working with his older partner Joe Pritchard in Cleveland.

❏ ❏ #1: Tonight I Said Goodbye
❏ ❏ #2: Sorrow's Anthem
❏ ❏ #3: A Welcome Grave
❏ ❏ #4: The Silent Hour
❏ ❏ # _____

Kozak, Harley Jane

Wollie Shelly: Greeting card artist Shelley runs into adventures in Los Angeles.

- ❏ ❏ #1: Dating Dead Men
- ❏ ❏ #2: Dating Is Murder
- ❏ ❏ #3: Dead Ex
- ❏ ❏ #4: A Date You Can't Refuse
- ❏ ❏ # _____

Kramer, Julie

Riley Spartz: As a television journalist, Spartz searches Minneapolis for stories that will translate into big ratings.

- ❏ ❏ #1: Stalking Susan
- ❏ ❏ #2: Missing Mark
- ❏ ❏ # _____

Krueger, William Kent

Cork O'Connor: O'Connor had a rough history in his small Minnesota town.

- ❏ ❏ #1: Iron Lake
- ❏ ❏ #2: Boundary Waters
- ❏ ❏ #3: Purgatory Ridge
- ❏ ❏ #4: Blood Hollow
- ❏ ❏ #5: Mercy Falls
- ❏ ❏ #6: Copper River
- ❏ ❏ #7: Thunder Bay
- ❏ ❏ #8: Red Knife
- ❏ ❏ #9: Heaven's Keep
- ❏ ❏ # _____

LAMB, JOHN J.

Bradley Lyon: Lyon is a retired San Francisco homicide detective. He and his wife Ashleigh have moved to Virginia's mountain country, where they have a teddy bear business.

❏ ❏ #1: The Mournful Teddy
❏ ❏ #2: The Crafty Teddy
❏ ❏ #3: The False-Hearted Teddy
❏ ❏ #4: The Clockwork Teddy
❏ ❏ #5: The Treacherous Teddy
❏ ❏ # _____

LANE, VICKI

Elizabeth Goodweather: After her husband died, Goodweather hoped to settle down with her flower business in North Carolina.

❏ ❏ #1: Signs in the Blood
❏ ❏ #2: Art's Blood
❏ ❏ #3: Old Wounds
❏ ❏ #4: In a Dark Season
❏ ❏ # _____

LAURIE, VICTORIA

Ghost Hunter: M.J. Holliday and her team track down ghosts and demons while also solving related mysteries.

❏ ❏ #1: What's a Ghoul to Do
❏ ❏ #2: Demons Are a Ghoul's Best Friend
❏ ❏ #3: Ghouls Just Haunt to Have Fun
❏ ❏ # _____

Psychic Eye: Abby Cooper works for the police as a psychic intuitive.

❏ ❏ #1: Abby Cooper: Psychic Eye

❏ ❏   #2: Better Read Than Dead
❏ ❏   #3: A Vision of Murder
❏ ❏   #4: Killer Insight
❏ ❏   #5: Crime Seen
❏ ❏   #6: Death Perception
❏ ❏   #7: Doom with a View
❏ ❏   # _____

Lavene, Joyce & Jim

Peggy Lee Garden: Lee is a botanist, widow of a detective, and the owner of garden shop in Charlotte called The Potting Shed.
❏ ❏   #1: Pretty Poison
❏ ❏   #2: Fruit of the Poisoned Tree
❏ ❏   #3: Poisoned Petals
❏ ❏   #4: Perfect Poison
❏ ❏   #5: A Corpse for Yew
❏ ❏   # _____

Renaissance Faire: Doctoral candidate Jessie Morton spends her summers at a renaissance faire in Columbia, South Carolina.
❏ ❏   #1: Wicked Weaves
❏ ❏   #2: Ghastly Glass
❏ ❏   # _____

Lawson, Mike

Joe De Marco: De Marco is a "fixer" for the Speaker of the House.
❏ ❏   #1: The Inside Ring
❏ ❏   #2: The Second Perimeter
❏ ❏   #3: House Rules
❏ ❏   #4: House Secrets
❏ ❏   # _____

LEHANE, DENNIS

Patrick Kenzie: Kenzie is a PI working in Boston with
his partner Angela Gennaro.

❏ ❏ #1: A Drink Before the War
❏ ❏ #2: Darkness, Take My Hand
❏ ❏ #3: Sacred
❏ ❏ #4: Gone, Baby, Gone
❏ ❏ #5: Prayers for Rain
❏ ❏ # _____

LEON, DONNA

Guido Brunetti: Set in the exotic city of Venice,
Brunetti works as the Commissario of Police.

❏ ❏ #1: Death at La Fenice
❏ ❏ #2: Death in a Strange Country
❏ ❏ #3: Dressed for Death
❏ ❏ #4: Death and Judgment
❏ ❏ #5: Acqua Alta
❏ ❏ #6: Quietly in Their Sleep
❏ ❏ #7: A Noble Radiance
❏ ❏ #8: Fatal Remedies
❏ ❏ #9: Friends in High Places
❏ ❏ #10: A Sea of Troubles
❏ ❏ #11: Wilful Behavior
❏ ❏ #12: Uniform Justice
❏ ❏ #13: Doctored Evidence
❏ ❏ #14: Blood from a Stone
❏ ❏ #15: Through a Glass Darkly
❏ ❏ #16: Suffer the Little Children
❏ ❏ #17: The Girl of His Dreams
❏ ❏ #18: About Face
❏ ❏ # _____

LESCROART, JOHN

Dismas Hardy: Hardy used to be a cop and is now a defense attorney and part owner of the Little Shamrock bar in San Francisco.

- ❏ ❏ #1: Dead Irish
- ❏ ❏ #2: The Vig
- ❏ ❏ #3: Hard Evidence
- ❏ ❏ #4: The 13th Juror
- ❏ ❏ #5: The Mercy Rule
- ❏ ❏ #6: Nothing But the Truth
- ❏ ❏ #7: The Oath
- ❏ ❏ #8: The First Law
- ❏ ❏ #9: The Motive
- ❏ ❏ #10: The Second Chair
- ❏ ❏ #11: The Suspect
- ❏ ❏ #12: Betrayal
- ❏ ❏ #13: A Plague of Secrets
- ❏ ❏ # _____

LEVINE, LAURA

Jaine Austen: Austen is a writer for hire, but doesn't seem to get paid for all of the murders she solves.

- ❏ ❏ #1: This Pen for Hire
- ❏ ❏ #2: Last Writes
- ❏ ❏ #3: Killer Blonde
- ❏ ❏ #4: Shoes to Die For
- ❏ ❏ #5: The PMS Murder
- ❏ ❏ #6: Death by Pantyhose
- ❏ ❏ #7: Killing Bridezilla
- ❏ ❏ #8: Killer Cruise
- ❏ ❏ # _____

LEVINE, PAUL

Solomon vs. Lord: Steve Solomon and Victoria
Lord are lawyers who work against each other in the
courtroom, but still manage to maintain a relationship.
- ❏ ❏ #1: Solomon Vs. Lord
- ❏ ❏ #2: The Deep Blue Alibi
- ❏ ❏ #3: Kill All the Lawyers
- ❏ ❏ #4: Trial & Error
- ❏ ❏ # _____

LEWIN, MICHAEL Z.

Albert Samson: Samson is a private detective based in
Indianapolis' Fountain Square neighborhood.
- ❏ ❏ #1: Ask the Right Question
- ❏ ❏ #2: The Way We Die Now
- ❏ ❏ #3: The Enemies Within
- ❏ ❏ #4: The Silent Salesman
- ❏ ❏ #5: Missing Woman
- ❏ ❏ #6: Out of Season
- ❏ ❏ #7: Called by a Panther
- ❏ ❏ #8: Eye Opener
- ❏ ❏ # _____

Leroy Powder: Powder is a veteran of the Indianapolis
police department.
- ❏ ❏ #1: Night Cover
- ❏ ❏ #2: Hard Line
- ❏ ❏ #3: Late Payments
- ❏ ❏ # _____

Lunghi Family: The Lunghis are three generations of
sleuths in Bath, England.
- ❏ ❏ #1: Family Business

❏ ❏ #2: Family Planning
❏ ❏ # _____

LIMÓN, MARTIN

George Sueno: Sueno and Ernie Bascom are detectives working in the Criminal Investigation Division of the US Army in Korea.
❏ ❏ #1: Jade Lady Burning
❏ ❏ #2: Slicky Boys
❏ ❏ #3: Buddha's Money
❏ ❏ #4: The Door to Bitterness
❏ ❏ #5: G.I. Bones
❏ ❏ # _____

LINDSAY, JEFF

Dexter Morgan: Morgan is a serial killer who has a code of ethics. He only kills "bad guys."
❏ ❏ #1: Darkly Dreaming Dexter
❏ ❏ #2: Dearly Devoted Dexter
❏ ❏ #3: Dexter in the Dark
❏ ❏ #4: Dexter by Design
❏ ❏ # _____

LIPPMAN, LAURA

Tess Monaghan: Monaghan used to be a reporter, but now she operates as a PI in Baltimore.
❏ ❏ #1: Baltimore Blues
❏ ❏ #2: Charm City
❏ ❏ #3: Butchers Hill
❏ ❏ #4: In Big Trouble
❏ ❏ #5: The Sugar House
❏ ❏ #6: In a Strange City
❏ ❏ #7: The Last Place

❏ ❏ #8: By a Spider's Thread
❏ ❏ #9: No Good Deeds
❏ ❏ #10: Another Thing to Fall
❏ ❏ # _____

Liss, David

Benjamin Weaver: Weaver is a Jew living in 18th century London, where he works as a boxer and an investigator.

❏ ❏ #1: A Conspiracy of Paper
❏ ❏ #2: A Spectacle of Corruption
❏ ❏ #3: The Devil's Company
❏ ❏ # _____

Lourey, Jess

Mira James: James used to live in the big city of Minneapolis, but now resides in rural Battle Lake, Minnesota.

❏ ❏ #1: May Day
❏ ❏ #2: June Bug
❏ ❏ #3: Knee High by the Fourth of July
❏ ❏ #4: August Moon
❏ ❏ #5: September Fair
❏ ❏ # _____

Lovesey, Peter

Hen Mallin: Mallin is a Senior Investigating Officer working in England.

❏ ❏ #1: The Circle
❏ ❏ #2: The Headhunters
❏ ❏ # _____

Peter Diamond: Detective Superintendent Diamond is a genuine gumshoe working in Bath.

- ❏ ❏ #1: The Last Detective
- ❏ ❏ #2: Diamond Solitaire
- ❏ ❏ #3: The Summons
- ❏ ❏ #4: Bloodhounds
- ❏ ❏ #5: Upon a Dark Night
- ❏ ❏ #6: The Vault
- ❏ ❏ #7: Diamond Dust
- ❏ ❏ #8: The House Sitter
- ❏ ❏ #9: The Secret Hangman
- ❏ ❏ #10: Skeleton Hill
- ❏ ❏ # _____

LUTZ, LISA

Spellman Files: A family of San Francisco private detectives who often use their skills to spy on each other.

- ❏ ❏ #1: The Spellman Files
- ❏ ❏ #2: Curse of the Spellmans
- ❏ ❏ #3: Revenge of the Spellmans
- ❏ ❏ # _____

MACBRIDE, STUART

Logan McRae: In Aberdeen, Scotland, McRae serves as a police detective.

- ❏ ❏ #1: Cold Granite
- ❏ ❏ #2: Dying Light
- ❏ ❏ #3: Bloodshot
- ❏ ❏ #4: Flesh House
- ❏ ❏ #5: Blind Eye
- ❏ ❏ # _____

MacInerney, Karen

Natalie Barnes: Natalie Barnes moved from Texas to
Maine to buy the Gray Whale Inn, a bed and breakfast
on Cranberry Island.

- ❏ ❏ #1: Murder on the Rocks
- ❏ ❏ #2: Dead and Berried
- ❏ ❏ #3: Murder Most Maine
- ❏ ❏ # _____

McGarrity, Michael

Kevin Kerney: Kerney used to be the chief of police in
Santa Fe.

- ❏ ❏ #1: Tularosa
- ❏ ❏ #2: Mexican Hat
- ❏ ❏ #3: Serpent Gate
- ❏ ❏ #4: Hermit's Peak
- ❏ ❏ #5: The Judas Judge
- ❏ ❏ #6: Under the Color of Law
- ❏ ❏ #7: The Big Gamble
- ❏ ❏ #8: Everyone Dies
- ❏ ❏ #9: Slow Kill
- ❏ ❏ #10: Nothing But Trouble
- ❏ ❏ #11: Death Song
- ❏ ❏ #12: Dead or Alive
- ❏ ❏ # _____

Maitland, Barry

Brock and Kolla: Detective Sergeant Kathy Kolla teams
up with Detective Chief Inspector David Brock of
Scotland Yard.

- ❏ ❏ #1: The Marx Sisters
- ❏ ❏ #2: The Malcontenta
- ❏ ❏ #3: All My Enemies

- ❏ ❏ #4: The Chalon Hands
- ❏ ❏ #5: Silvermeadow
- ❏ ❏ #6: Babel
- ❏ ❏ #7: The Verge Practice
- ❏ ❏ #8: No Trace
- ❏ ❏ #9: Spider Trap
- ❏ ❏ #10: Dark Mirror
- ❏ ❏ # _____

MANKELL, HENNING

Kurt Wallander: Wallander is a police officer working in Ystad, Sweden, where he struggles with alcohol and anger.

- ❏ ❏ #1: Faceless Killers
- ❏ ❏ #2: The Dogs of Riga
- ❏ ❏ #3: The White Lioness
- ❏ ❏ #4: The Man Who Smiled
- ❏ ❏ #5: Sidetracked
- ❏ ❏ #6: The Fifth Woman
- ❏ ❏ #7: One Step Behind
- ❏ ❏ #8: Firewall
- ❏ ❏ # _____

MARON, MARGARET

Deborah Knott: Knott is a judge in Colleton County, North Carolina, home to her large family and its colorful past.

- ❏ ❏ #1: Bootlegger's Daughter
- ❏ ❏ #2: Southern Discomfort
- ❏ ❏ #3: Shooting at Loons
- ❏ ❏ #4: Up Jumps the Devil
- ❏ ❏ #5: Killer Market
- ❏ ❏ #6: Home Fires

❏ ❏ #7: Storm Track
❏ ❏ #8: Uncommon Clay
❏ ❏ #9: Slow Dollar
❏ ❏ #10: High Country Fall
❏ ❏ #11: Rituals of the Season
❏ ❏ #12: Winter's Child
❏ ❏ #13: Hard Row
❏ ❏ #14: Death's Half Acre
❏ ❏ #15: Sand Sharks
❏ ❏ # _____

MARTIN, ANDREW

Jim Stringer: Stringer is a railway porter who is reassigned to the North Eastern Railway Police in Edwardian England.
❏ ❏ #1: The Necropolis Railway
❏ ❏ #2: The Blackpool Highflyer
❏ ❏ #3: The Lost Luggage Porter
❏ ❏ #4: Murder at Deviation Junction
❏ ❏ # _____

MARTIN, NANCY

Blackbird Sisters: Nora Blackbird and her sisters investigate mysteries in Philadelphia society.
❏ ❏ #1: How to Murder a Millionaire
❏ ❏ #2: Dead Girls Don't Wear Diamonds
❏ ❏ #3: Some Like It Lethal
❏ ❏ #4: Cross Your Heart and Hope to Die
❏ ❏ #5: Have Your Cake and Kill Him Too
❏ ❏ #6: A Crazy Little Thing Called Death
❏ ❏ #7: Murder Melts in Your Mouth
❏ ❏ # _____

MAY, PETER

Enzo Files: Enzo Macleod is a biologist who travels around France interpreting murders while using forensics.

- ❏ ❏ #1: Extraordinary People
- ❏ ❏ #2: The Critic
- ❏ ❏ #3: Blacklight Blue
- ❏ ❏ # _____

MAYOR, ARCHER

Joe Gunther: Lieutenant Gunther is the lead detective in the Brattleboro, Vermont, police department.

- ❏ ❏ #1: Open Season
- ❏ ❏ #2: Borderlines
- ❏ ❏ #3: Scent of Evil
- ❏ ❏ #4: The Skeleton's Knee
- ❏ ❏ #5: Fruits of the Poisonous Tree
- ❏ ❏ #6: The Dark Root
- ❏ ❏ #7: The Ragman's Memory
- ❏ ❏ #8: Bellows Falls
- ❏ ❏ #9: The Disposable Man
- ❏ ❏ #10: Occam's Razor
- ❏ ❏ #11: The Marble Mask
- ❏ ❏ #12: Tucker Peak
- ❏ ❏ #13: The Sniper's Wife
- ❏ ❏ #14: Gatekeeper
- ❏ ❏ #15: The Surrogate Thief
- ❏ ❏ #16: St. Alban's Fire
- ❏ ❏ #17: The Second Mouse
- ❏ ❏ #18: Chat
- ❏ ❏ #19: The Catch
- ❏ ❏ #20: The Price of Malice
- ❏ ❏ # _____

McBride, Susan

Andy Kendricks: Dallas heiress Kendricks would rather be a website designer instead of a Junior League member.

- ❏ ❏ #1: Blue Blood
- ❏ ❏ #2: The Good Girl's Guide to Murder
- ❏ ❏ #3: The Lone Star Lonely Hearts Club
- ❏ ❏ #4: Night of the Living Deb
- ❏ ❏ #5: Too Pretty to Die
- ❏ ❏ # _____

McDermid, Val

Tony Hill: Clinical psychologist Hill suffers from sexual dysfunction and profiles serial killers.

- ❏ ❏ #1: The Mermaids Singing
- ❏ ❏ #2: The Wire in the Blood
- ❏ ❏ #3: The Last Temptation
- ❏ ❏ #4: The Torment of Others
- ❏ ❏ #5: Beneath the Bleeding
- ❏ ❏ # _____

McIntosh, Pat

Gilbert Cunningham: Cunningham is a lawyer who solves murders in medieval Scotland.

- ❏ ❏ #1: The Harper's Quine
- ❏ ❏ #2: The Nicholas Feast
- ❏ ❏ #3: The Merchant's Mark
- ❏ ❏ #4: St. Mungo's Robin
- ❏ ❏ #5: The Rough Collier
- ❏ ❏ #6: The Stolen Voice
- ❏ ❏ # _____

MEIER, LESLIE

Lucy Stone: Stone solves murders and takes care of her family in the small town of Tinker's Cove, Maine.

- ❏ ❏ #1: Mistletoe Murder
- ❏ ❏ #2: Tippy-Toe Murder
- ❏ ❏ #3: Trick or Treat Murder
- ❏ ❏ #4: Back to School Murder
- ❏ ❏ #5: Valentine Murder
- ❏ ❏ #6: Christmas Cookie Murder
- ❏ ❏ #7: Turkey Day Murder
- ❏ ❏ #8: Wedding Day Murder
- ❏ ❏ #9: Birthday Party Murder
- ❏ ❏ #10: Father's Day Murder
- ❏ ❏ #11: Star Spangled Murder
- ❏ ❏ #12: New Year's Eve Murder
- ❏ ❏ #13: Bake Sale Murder
- ❏ ❏ #14: St. Patrick's Day Murder
- ❏ ❏ #15: Mother's Day Murder
- ❏ ❏ # _____

MILLER, JOHN RAMSEY

Winter Massey: Massey is a former US Marshal with a young son who is blind.

- ❏ ❏ #1: Inside Out
- ❏ ❏ #2: Upside Down
- ❏ ❏ #3: Side by Side
- ❏ ❏ #4: Smoke & Mirrors
- ❏ ❏ # _____

MILLER, SUSAN CUMMINS

Frankie MacFarlane: MacFarlane is a geologist working in Nevada.

- ❏ ❏ #1: Death Assemblage

❏ ❏ #2: Detachment Fault

❏ ❏ #3: Quarry

❏ ❏ #4: Hoodoo

❏ ❏ # _____

Mosley, Walter

Easy Rawlins: In a series that spans three decades
(1948 to 1967), Rawlins confronts the landscape of race
relations in Los Angeles.

❏ ❏ #1: Devil in a Blue Dress

❏ ❏ #2: A Red Death

❏ ❏ #3: White Butterfly

❏ ❏ #4: Black Betty

❏ ❏ #5: A Little Yellow Dog

❏ ❏ #6: Gone Fishin'

❏ ❏ #7: Bad Boy Brawly Brown

❏ ❏ #8: Six Easy Pieces

❏ ❏ #9: Little Scarlet

❏ ❏ #10: Cinnamon Kiss

❏ ❏ #11: Blonde Faith

❏ ❏ # _____

Fearless Jones: Along with his friend Paris Minton,
Jones fights crime in 1950s Los Angeles.

❏ ❏ #1: Fearless Jones

❏ ❏ #2: Fear Itself

❏ ❏ #3: Fear of the Dark

❏ ❏ # _____

Socrates Fortlow: After being imprisoned for twenty-
seven years, Fortlow returns to the world with a new
perspective.

❏ ❏ #1: Always Outnumbered, Always Outgunned

❏ ❏ #2: Walkin' the Dog

❑ ❑ #3: The Right Mistake
❑ ❑ # _____

MULLER, MARCIA

Sharon McCone: In San Francisco, Sharon McCone
begins her career as an investigator for a legal
cooperative before striking out to work independently.

❑ ❑ #1: Edwin of the Iron Shoes
❑ ❑ #2: Ask the Cards a Question
❑ ❑ #3: The Cheshire Cat's Eye
❑ ❑ #4: Games to Keep the Dark Away
❑ ❑ #5: Leave a Message for Willie
❑ ❑ #6: Double (with Bill Pronzini)
❑ ❑ #7: There's Nothing to Be Afraid Of
❑ ❑ #8: Eye of the Storm
❑ ❑ #9: There's Something in a Sunday
❑ ❑ #10: The Shape of Dread
❑ ❑ #11: Trophies and Dead Things
❑ ❑ #12: Where Echoes Live
❑ ❑ #13: Pennies on a Dead Woman's Eyes
❑ ❑ #14: Wolf in the Shadows
❑ ❑ #15: Till the Butchers Cut Him Down
❑ ❑ #16: A Wild and Lonely Place
❑ ❑ #17: The Broken Promise Land
❑ ❑ #18: Both Ends of the Night
❑ ❑ #19: While Other People Sleep
❑ ❑ #20: A Walk Through the Fire
❑ ❑ #21: Listen to the Silence
❑ ❑ #22: Dead Midnight
❑ ❑ #23: The Dangerous Hour
❑ ❑ #24: Vanishing Point
❑ ❑ #25: The Ever-Running Man
❑ ❑ #26: Burn Out

❏ ❏   #27: Locked In
❏ ❏   # _____

MURPHY, SHIRLEY ROUSSEAU

Joe Grey: Joe is a talking cat who has mastered the
English language.

❏ ❏   #1: Cat on the Edge
❏ ❏   #2: Cat Under Fire
❏ ❏   #3: Cat Raise the Dead
❏ ❏   #4: Cat in the Dark
❏ ❏   #5: Cat to the Dogs
❏ ❏   #6: Cat Spitting Mad
❏ ❏   #7: Cat Laughing Last
❏ ❏   #8: Cat Seeing Double
❏ ❏   #9: Cat Fear No Evil
❏ ❏   #10: Cat Cross Their Graves
❏ ❏   #11: Cat Breaking Free
❏ ❏   #12: Cat Pay the Devil
❏ ❏   #13: Cat Deck the Halls
❏ ❏   #14: Cat Playing Cupid
❏ ❏   #15: Cat Striking Back
❏ ❏   # _____

MYERS, BEVERLE GRAVES

Tito Amato: In 18th century Venice, Amato is a castrato
opera singer.

❏ ❏   #1: Interrupted Aria
❏ ❏   #2: Painted Veil
❏ ❏   #3: Cruel Music
❏ ❏   #4: The Iron Tongue of Midnight
❏ ❏   #5: Her Deadly Mischief
❏ ❏   # _____

MYERS, TAMAR

Abigail Timberlake: Timberlake owns the Den of Antiquity, an antiques store where objects lead to mysteries.

- ❏ ❏ #1: Larceny and Old Lace
- ❏ ❏ #2: Gilt By Association
- ❏ ❏ #3: The Ming and I
- ❏ ❏ #4: So Faux So Good
- ❏ ❏ #5: Baroque and Desperate
- ❏ ❏ #6: Estate of Mind
- ❏ ❏ #7: A Penny Urned
- ❏ ❏ #8: Nightmare in Shining Armor
- ❏ ❏ #9: Splendor in the Glass
- ❏ ❏ #10: Tiles and Tribulations
- ❏ ❏ #11: Statue of Limitations
- ❏ ❏ #12: Monet Talks
- ❏ ❏ #13: The Cane Mutiny
- ❏ ❏ #14: Death of a Rug Lord
- ❏ ❏ #15: Poison Ivory
- ❏ ❏ # _____

Magdalena Yoder: Yoder runs the Pennsylvania Dutch Inn where customers leave happy or dead.

- ❏ ❏ #1: Too Many Crooks Spoil the Broth
- ❏ ❏ #2: Parsley, Sage, Rosemary and Crime
- ❏ ❏ #3: No Use Dying Over Spilled Milk
- ❏ ❏ #4: Just Plain Pickled to Death
- ❏ ❏ #5: Between a Wok and a Hard Place
- ❏ ❏ #6: Eat, Drink, and Be Wary
- ❏ ❏ #7: Play It Again, Spam
- ❏ ❏ #8: The Hand That Rocks the Ladle
- ❏ ❏ #9: The Crepes of Wrath
- ❏ ❏ #10: Gruel and Unusual Punishment
- ❏ ❏ #11: Custard's Last Stand

❏ ❏ #12: Thou Shalt Not Grill
❏ ❏ #13: Assault and Pepper
❏ ❏ #14: Grape Expectations
❏ ❏ #15: Hell Hath No Curry
❏ ❏ #16: As the World Churns
❏ ❏ #17: Batter Off Dead
❏ ❏ # _____

NADEL, BARBARA

Cetin Ikmen: Inspector Ikmen investigates murders throughout the exotic city of Istanbul.
❏ ❏ #1: Belshazzar's Daughter
❏ ❏ #2: The Ottoman Cage
❏ ❏ #3: Arabesk
❏ ❏ # _____

NEWMAN, SHARAN

Catherine LeVendeur: LeVendeur is a young scholar at the Convent of the Paraclete in France during the 12th century.
❏ ❏ #1: Death Comes as Epiphany
❏ ❏ #2: The Devil's Door
❏ ❏ #3: The Wandering Arm
❏ ❏ #4: Strong as Death
❏ ❏ #5: Cursed in the Blood
❏ ❏ #6: The Difficult Saint
❏ ❏ #7: To Wear the White Cloak
❏ ❏ #8: Heresy
❏ ❏ #9: The Outcast Dove
❏ ❏ #10: The Witch in the Well
❏ ❏ # _____

O'CONNELL, CAROL

Kathleen Mallory: Mallory used to live on the streets but now she is now a New York City police detective.

- ❏ ❏ #1: Mallory's Oracle
- ❏ ❏ #2: The Man Who Cast Two Shadows
- ❏ ❏ #3: Killing Critics
- ❏ ❏ #4: Stone Angel
- ❏ ❏ #5: Shell Game
- ❏ ❏ #6: Crime School
- ❏ ❏ #7: Dead Famous
- ❏ ❏ #8: Winter House
- ❏ ❏ #9: Find Me
- ❏ ❏ # _____

PAGE, KATHERINE HALL

Faith Fairchild: In the sleepy Massachusetts village of Aleford, Fairchild is a caterer and minister's wife.

- ❏ ❏ #1: The Body in the Belfry
- ❏ ❏ #2: The Body in the Kelp
- ❏ ❏ #3: The Body in the Bouillon
- ❏ ❏ #4: The Body in the Vestibule
- ❏ ❏ #5: The Body in the Cast
- ❏ ❏ #6: The Body in the Basement
- ❏ ❏ #7: The Body in the Bog
- ❏ ❏ #8: The Body in the Fjord
- ❏ ❏ #9: The Body in the Bookcase
- ❏ ❏ #10: The Body in the Big Apple
- ❏ ❏ #11: The Body in the Moonlight
- ❏ ❏ #12: The Body in the Bonfire
- ❏ ❏ #13: The Body in the Lighthouse
- ❏ ❏ #14: The Body in the Attic
- ❏ ❏ #15: The Body in the Snowdrift
- ❏ ❏ #16: The Body in the Ivy
- ❏ ❏ #17: The Body in the Gallery

❑ ❑ #18: The Body in the Sleigh
❑ ❑ # _____

PARETSKY, SARA

V.I. Warshawski: Warshawski is a Chicago private eye whose cases often involve white collar crime.
❑ ❑ #1: Indemnity Only
❑ ❑ #2: Deadlock
❑ ❑ #3: Killing Orders
❑ ❑ #4: Bitter Medicine
❑ ❑ #5: Blood Shot
❑ ❑ #6: Burn Marks
❑ ❑ #7: Guardian Angel
❑ ❑ #8: Tunnel Vision
❑ ❑ #9: Hard Time
❑ ❑ #10: Total Recall
❑ ❑ #11: Blacklist
❑ ❑ #12: Fire Sale
❑ ❑ #13: Hardball
❑ ❑ # _____

PARKER, ROBERT B.

Jesse Stone: Stone had a history of baseball and alcoholism before he became the police chief in Paradise, Massachusetts.
❑ ❑ #1: Night Passage
❑ ❑ #2: Trouble in Paradise
❑ ❑ #3: Death in Paradise
❑ ❑ #4: Stone Cold
❑ ❑ #5: Sea Change
❑ ❑ #6: High Profile
❑ ❑ #7: Stranger in Paradise
❑ ❑ #8: Night and Day
❑ ❑ # _____

Spenser: Spenser and his partner Hawk used to be boxers, but now work in Boston as PIs.

❏ ❏ #1: The Godwulf Manuscript
❏ ❏ #2: God Save the Child
❏ ❏ #3: Mortal Stakes
❏ ❏ #4: Promised Land
❏ ❏ #5: The Judas Goat
❏ ❏ #6: Looking for Rachel Wallace
❏ ❏ #7: Early Autumn
❏ ❏ #8: A Savage Place
❏ ❏ #9: Ceremony
❏ ❏ #10: The Widening Gyre
❏ ❏ #11: Valediction
❏ ❏ #12: A Catskill Eagle
❏ ❏ #13: Taming a Sea-Horse
❏ ❏ #14: Pale Kings and Princes
❏ ❏ #15: Crimson Joy
❏ ❏ #16: Playmates
❏ ❏ #17: Stardust
❏ ❏ #18: Pastime
❏ ❏ #19: Double Deuce
❏ ❏ #20: Paper Doll
❏ ❏ #21: Walking Shadow
❏ ❏ #22: Thin Air
❏ ❏ #23: Chance
❏ ❏ #24: Small Vices
❏ ❏ #25: Sudden Mischief
❏ ❏ #26: Hush Money
❏ ❏ #27: Hugger Mugger
❏ ❏ #27: Potshot
❏ ❏ #29: Widow's Walk
❏ ❏ #30: Back Story
❏ ❏ #31: Bad Business
❏ ❏ #32: Cold Service

❏ ❏ #33: School Days
❏ ❏ #34: Hundred-Dollar Baby
❏ ❏ #35: Now and Then
❏ ❏ #36: Rough Weather
❏ ❏ #37: The Professional
❏ ❏ # _____

Sunny Randall: Randall is a PI in Boston, who unlike Parker's other series protagonists, does not possess a Y chromosome.
❏ ❏ #1: Family Honor
❏ ❏ #2: Perish Twice
❏ ❏ #3: Shrink Rap
❏ ❏ #4: Melancholy Baby
❏ ❏ #5: Blue Screen
❏ ❏ #6: Spare Change
❏ ❏ # _____

Virgil Cole: Cole and Everett Hitch are cowboys in the Old West.
❏ ❏ #1: Appaloosa
❏ ❏ #2: Resolution
❏ ❏ #3: Brimstone
❏ ❏ # _____

PARRISH, P.J.

Louis Kincaid: "A beat-down former Detroit cop of mixed race heads home to the South, and finds trouble everywhere he goes," says Mystery Scene magazine.
❏ ❏ #1: Dark of the Moon
❏ ❏ #2: Dead of Winter
❏ ❏ #3: Paint it Black
❏ ❏ #4: Thicker Than Water
❏ ❏ #5: Island of Bones

❏ ❏ #6: A Killing Rain
❏ ❏ #7: Unquiet Grave
❏ ❏ #8: A Thousand Bones
❏ ❏ #9: South of Hell
❏ ❏ #10: The Little Death
❏ ❏ # _____

PATTERSON, JAMES

Alex Cross: Cross is an expert in catching the most vicious serial killers.
❏ ❏ #1: Along Came a Spider
❏ ❏ #2: Kiss the Girls
❏ ❏ #3: Jack and Jill
❏ ❏ #4: Cat & Mouse
❏ ❏ #5: Pop Goes the Weasel
❏ ❏ #6: Roses Are Red
❏ ❏ #7: Violets Are Blue
❏ ❏ #8: Four Blind Mice
❏ ❏ #9: Big Bad Wolf
❏ ❏ #10: London Bridges
❏ ❏ #11: Mary, Mary
❏ ❏ #12: Cross
❏ ❏ #13: Double Cross
❏ ❏ #14: Cross Country
❏ ❏ #15: Alex Cross's Trial (w/Richard DiLallo)
❏ ❏ #16: I, Alex Cross
❏ ❏ # _____

Women's Murder Club: Each woman in this club is equipped with a certain set of skills that help her figure out murders in the area.
❏ ❏ #1: 1st to Die
❏ ❏ #2: 2nd Chance (with Andrew Gross)

❏ ❏ #3: 3rd Degree (with Andrew Gross)
❏ ❏ #4: 4th of July (with Maxine Paetro)
❏ ❏ #5: The 5th Horseman (with Maxine Paetro)
❏ ❏ #6: The 6th Target (with Maxine Paetro)
❏ ❏ #7: 7th Heaven (with Maxine Paetro)
❏ ❏ #8: 8th Confession (with Maxine Paetro)
❏ ❏ # _____

PATTISON, ELIOT

Inspector Shan: Veteran police inspector Shan Tao Yun
unravels murders in Beijing.
❏ ❏ #1: The Skull Mantra
❏ ❏ #2: Water Touching Stone
❏ ❏ #3: Bone Mountain
❏ ❏ #4: Beautiful Ghosts
❏ ❏ #5: Prayer of the Dragon
❏ ❏ #6: The Lord of Death
❏ ❏ # _____

PENNY, LOUISE

Armand Gamache: Chief Inspector Gamache travels to
the small town of Three Pines to solve murders more
often than you'd think likely for such an idyllic place.
❏ ❏ #1: Still Life
❏ ❏ #2: A Fatal Grace
❏ ❏ #3: The Cruelest Month
❏ ❏ #4: A Rule Against Murder
❏ ❏ #5: The Brutal Telling
❏ ❏ # _____

Perona, Tony

Nick Bertetto: Indiana freelance writer and family man Bertetto investigates cases that involve faith and murder.

❏ ❏ #1: Second Advent
❏ ❏ #2: Angels Whisper
❏ ❏ # _____

Perry, Thomas

Jane Whitefield: Whitefield is a Native American "guide" who can help people disappear.

❏ ❏ #1: Vanishing Act
❏ ❏ #2: Dance for the Dead
❏ ❏ #3: Shadow Woman
❏ ❏ #4: The Face-Changers
❏ ❏ #5: Blood Money
❏ ❏ #6: Runner
❏ ❏ # _____

Peters, Elizabeth

Amelia Peabody: Victorian feminist Peabody travels to Egypt to fulfill her dream of excavating archaeological sites.

❏ ❏ #1: Crocodile on the Sandbank
❏ ❏ #2: The Curse of the Pharaohs
❏ ❏ #3: The Mummy Case
❏ ❏ #4: Lion in the Valley
❏ ❏ #5: The Deeds of the Disturber
❏ ❏ #6: The Last Camel Died at Noon
❏ ❏ #7: The Snake, the Crocodile and the Dog
❏ ❏ #8: The Hippopotamus Pool
❏ ❏ #9: Seeing a Large Cat
❏ ❏ #10: The Ape Who Guards the Balance

❏ ❏ #11: The Falcon at the Portal
❏ ❏ #12: Thunder in the Sky
❏ ❏ #13: Lord of the Silent
❏ ❏ #14: The Golden One
❏ ❏ #15: Children of the Storm
❏ ❏ #16: Guardian of the Horizon
❏ ❏ #17: The Serpent on the Crown
❏ ❏ #18: Tomb of the Golden Bird
❏ ❏ # _____

PHELAN, TWIST

Pinnacle Peak: In Pinnacle Peak, Arizona, attorney
Hannah Dain solves sports related mysteries.

❏ ❏ #1: Heir Apparent
❏ ❏ #2: Family Claims
❏ ❏ #3: Spurred Ambition
❏ ❏ #4: False Fortune
❏ ❏ # _____

PICKARD, NANCY

Jenny Cain: Cain is the director of the Port Frederick
Civic Foundation in Massachusetts.

❏ ❏ #1: Generous Death
❏ ❏ #2: Say No to Murder
❏ ❏ #3: No Body
❏ ❏ #4: Marriage Is Murder
❏ ❏ #5: Dead Crazy
❏ ❏ #6: Bum Steer
❏ ❏ #7: I.O.U.
❏ ❏ #8: But I Wouldn't Want to Die There
❏ ❏ #9: Confession
❏ ❏ #10: Twilight
❏ ❏ # _____

Marie Lightfoot: Lightfoot is a writer of true-crime books whose work attracts the interest of the killers she writes about.

- ❏ ❏ #1: The Whole Truth
- ❏ ❏ #2: Ring of Truth
- ❏ ❏ #3: The Truth Hurts
- ❏ ❏ # _____

PICKENS, CATHY

Avery Andrews: Andrews used to be a big-shot attorney in the city, but now enjoys a simpler life in Dacus, South Carolina.

- ❏ ❏ #1: Southern Fried
- ❏ ❏ #2: Done Gone Wrong
- ❏ ❏ #3: Hog Wild
- ❏ ❏ #4: Hush My Mouth
- ❏ ❏ #5: Can't Never Tell
- ❏ ❏ # _____

PRESTON, DOUGLAS & CHILD, LINCOLN

Pendergast: Pendergast is a special agent working for the FBI to track down serial killers, often in New York.

- ❏ ❏ #1: The Relic
- ❏ ❏ #2: Reliquary
- ❏ ❏ #3: The Cabinet of Curiosities
- ❏ ❏ #4: Still Life with Crows
- ❏ ❏ #5: Brimstone
- ❏ ❏ #6: The Dance of Death
- ❏ ❏ #7: The Book of the Dead
- ❏ ❏ #8: The Wheel of Darkness
- ❏ ❏ #9: Cemetery Dance
- ❏ ❏ # _____

Pronzini, Bill

Nameless Detective: This nameless detective works in San Francisco taking cases with his partner Eberhardt.

- ❏ ❏ #1: The Snatch
- ❏ ❏ #2: The Vanished
- ❏ ❏ #3: Undercurrent
- ❏ ❏ #4: Blowback
- ❏ ❏ #5: Twospot (with Collin Wilcox)
- ❏ ❏ #6: Labyrinth
- ❏ ❏ #7: Hoodwink
- ❏ ❏ #8: Scattershot
- ❏ ❏ #9: Dragonfire
- ❏ ❏ #10: Bindlestiff
- ❏ ❏ #11: Double (with Marcia Muller)
- ❏ ❏ #12: Nightshades
- ❏ ❏ #13: Quicksilver
- ❏ ❏ #14: Bones
- ❏ ❏ #15: Deadfall
- ❏ ❏ #16: Shackles
- ❏ ❏ #17: Jackpot
- ❏ ❏ #18: Breakdown
- ❏ ❏ #19: Quarry
- ❏ ❏ #20: Epitaphs
- ❏ ❏ #21: Demons
- ❏ ❏ #22: Hardcase
- ❏ ❏ #23: Sentinels
- ❏ ❏ #24: Illusions
- ❏ ❏ #26: Crazybone
- ❏ ❏ #27: Bleeders
- ❏ ❏ #28: Spook
- ❏ ❏ #29: Scenarios
- ❏ ❏ #30: Nightcrawlers
- ❏ ❏ #31: Mourners
- ❏ ❏ #32: Savages

❏ ❏   #33: Fever
❏ ❏   #34: Schemers
❏ ❏   # _____

PURSER, ANN

Lois Meade: Meade is a cleaner in the English village of Long Farnden.
❏ ❏   #1: Murder on Monday
❏ ❏   #2: Terror on Tuesday
❏ ❏   #3: Weeping on Wednesday
❏ ❏   #4: Theft on Thursday
❏ ❏   #5: Fear on Friday
❏ ❏   #6: Secrets on Saturday
❏ ❏   #7: Sorrow on Sunday
❏ ❏   #8: Warning at One
❏ ❏   #9: Tragedy at Two
❏ ❏   # _____

RANKIN, IAN

John Rebus: Inspector Rebus is a police detective who operates around Edinburgh.
❏ ❏   #1: Knots and Crosses
❏ ❏   #2: Hide and Seek
❏ ❏   #3: Tooth and Nail
❏ ❏   #4: Strip Jack
❏ ❏   #5: The Black Book
❏ ❏   #6: Mortal Causes
❏ ❏   #7: Let It Bleed
❏ ❏   #8: Black and Blue
❏ ❏   #9: The Hanging Garden
❏ ❏   #10: Dead Souls
❏ ❏   #11: Set in Darkness
❏ ❏   #12: The Falls
❏ ❏   #13: Resurrection Men

❑ ❑ #14: A Question of Blood
❑ ❑ #15: Fleshmarket Alley
❑ ❑ #16: The Naming of the Dead
❑ ❑ #17: Exit Music
❑ ❑ # _____

Raybourn, Deanna

Lady Julia Grey: In Victorian London society, Lady
Grey investigates murders … quietly.
❑ ❑ #1: Silent in the Grave
❑ ❑ #2: Silent in the Sanctuary
❑ ❑ #3: Silent on the Moor
❑ ❑ # _____

Reed, Mary & Eric Mayer

John the Eunuch: In the 6th century of the Roman
Empire, John the Eunuch solves crimes numerically.
❑ ❑ #1: One for Sorrow
❑ ❑ #2: Two for Joy
❑ ❑ #3: Three for a Letter
❑ ❑ #4: Four for a Boy
❑ ❑ #5: Five for Silver
❑ ❑ #6: Six for Gold
❑ ❑ #7: Seven for a Secret
❑ ❑ # _____

Rees, Matt Beynon

Omar Yussef: Working as a teacher in Palestinian
territories, Yussef can't avoid corruption and murder.
❑ ❑ #1: The Collaborator of Bethlehem
❑ ❑ #2: A Grave in Gaza
❑ ❑ #3: The Samaritan's Secret
❑ ❑ # _____

Reichs, Kathy

Temperance Brennan: Dr. Brennan is a forensic anthropologist who works at the Laboratoire de Medecine Legale in Montreal and also in North Carolina.

- ❏ ❏ #1: Deja Dead
- ❏ ❏ #2: Death du Jour
- ❏ ❏ #3: Deadly Decisions
- ❏ ❏ #4: Fatal Voyage
- ❏ ❏ #5: Grave Secrets
- ❏ ❏ #6: Bare Bones
- ❏ ❏ #7: Monday Mourning
- ❏ ❏ #8: Cross Bones
- ❏ ❏ #9: Break No Bones
- ❏ ❏ #10: Bones to Ashes
- ❏ ❏ #11: Devil Bones
- ❏ ❏ #12: 206 Bones
- ❏ ❏ # _____

Rendell, Ruth

Reginald Wexford: Inspector Wexford teams with the straight-laced Mike Burden to solve crimes, often among families.

- ❏ ❏ #1: From Doon with Death
- ❏ ❏ #2: Sins of the Fathers
- ❏ ❏ #3: Wolf to the Slaughter
- ❏ ❏ #4: The Best Man to Die
- ❏ ❏ #5: A Guilty Thing Surprised
- ❏ ❏ #6: No More Dying Then
- ❏ ❏ #7: Murder Being Once Done
- ❏ ❏ #8: Some Lie and Some Die
- ❏ ❏ #9: Shake Hands Forever
- ❏ ❏ #10: A Sleeping Life
- ❏ ❏ #11: Death Notes

❏ ❏ #12: The Speaker of Mandarin
❏ ❏ #13: An Unkindness of Ravens
❏ ❏ #14: The Veiled One
❏ ❏ #15: Kissing the Gunner's Daughter
❏ ❏ #16: Simisola
❏ ❏ #17: Road Rage
❏ ❏ #18: Harm Done
❏ ❏ #19: The Babes in the Wood
❏ ❏ #20: End in Tears
❏ ❏ #21: Not in the Flesh
❏ ❏ #22: The Monster in the Box
❏ ❏ # _____

RICHARDS, EMILIE

Aggie Sloan-Wilcox: Sloan-Wilcox is the wife of a
Unitarian minister in Ohio.
❏ ❏ #1: Blessed Be the Busybody
❏ ❏ #2: Let There Be Suspects
❏ ❏ #3: Beware False Profits
❏ ❏ #4: A Lie for a Lie
❏ ❏ # _____

ROBB, CANDACE

Owen Archer: During the 14th century, Archer
works with his wife Lucie Wilton, an apothecary, to
investigate mysteries set in York.
❏ ❏ #1: The Apothecary Rose
❏ ❏ #2: The Lady Chapel
❏ ❏ #3: The Nun's Tale
❏ ❏ #4: The King's Bishop
❏ ❏ #5: The Riddle of St. Leonard's
❏ ❏ #6: A Gift of Sanctuary
❏ ❏ #7: A Spy for the Redeemer
❏ ❏ #8: The Cross-Legged Knight

❏ ❏ #9: The Guilt of Innocents
❏ ❏ #10: A Vigil of Spies
❏ ❏ # _____

ROBB, J.D.

Eve Dallas: Dallas is a police lieutenant in New York City who learns that everything ends IN DEATH!

❏ ❏ #1: Naked in Death
❏ ❏ #2: Glory in Death
❏ ❏ #3: Immortal in Death
❏ ❏ #4: Rapture in Death
❏ ❏ #5: Ceremony in Death
❏ ❏ #6: Vengeance in Death
❏ ❏ #7: Holiday in Death
❏ ❏ #8: Conspiracy in Death
❏ ❏ #9: Loyalty in Death
❏ ❏ #10: Witness in Death
❏ ❏ #11: Judgment in Death
❏ ❏ #12: Betrayal in Death
❏ ❏ #13: Seduction in Death
❏ ❏ #14: Reunion in Death
❏ ❏ #15: Purity in Death
❏ ❏ #16: Portrait in Death
❏ ❏ #17: Imitation in Death
❏ ❏ #18: Divided in Death
❏ ❏ #19: Visions in Death
❏ ❏ #20: Survivor in Death
❏ ❏ #21: Origin in Death
❏ ❏ #22: Memory in Death
❏ ❏ #23: Born in Death
❏ ❏ #24: Innocent in Death
❏ ❏ #25: Creation in Death
❏ ❏ #26: Strangers in Death
❏ ❏ #27: Salvation in Death

❏ ❏ #28: Promises in Death
❏ ❏ #29: Kindred in Death
❏ ❏ # _____

ROBERTS, NATALIE M.

Jenny T. Partridge: Partridge runs a dance school in
Utah where she deals with death and prima donnas.
❏ ❏ #1: Tutu Deadly
❏ ❏ #2: Tapped Out
❏ ❏ #3: Pointe and Shoot
❏ ❏ # _____

ROBINSON, PETER

Alan Banks: Detective Chief Inspector Banks moved to
Yorkshire from London to escape the stress of city life.
❏ ❏ #1: Gallows View
❏ ❏ #2: A Dedicated Man
❏ ❏ #3: A Necessary End
❏ ❏ #4: The Hanging Valley
❏ ❏ #5: Past Reason Hated
❏ ❏ #6: Wednesday's Child
❏ ❏ #7: Final Account
❏ ❏ #8: Innocent Graves
❏ ❏ #9: Blood at the Root
❏ ❏ #10: In a Dry Season
❏ ❏ #11: Cold Is the Grave
❏ ❏ #12: Aftermath
❏ ❏ #13: Close to Home
❏ ❏ #14: Playing with Fire
❏ ❏ #15: Strange Affair
❏ ❏ #16: Piece of My Heart
❏ ❏ #17: Friend of the Devil
❏ ❏ #18: All the Colors of Darkness
❏ ❏ # _____

Rosenfelt, David

Andy Carpenter: Carpenter is a defense attorney who figures out his cases with the help of his girlfriend and his beloved golden retriever, Tara.

❏ ❏ #1: Open and Shut
❏ ❏ #2: First Degree
❏ ❏ #3: Bury the Lead
❏ ❏ #4: Sudden Death
❏ ❏ #5: Dead Center
❏ ❏ #6: Play Dead
❏ ❏ #7: New Tricks
❏ ❏ # _____

Rowe, Rosemary

Libertus: Roman detective Libertus is a mosaicist in Roman Britain, which makes him an expert in puzzles and patterns—good for piecing together mysteries.

❏ ❏ #1: The Germanicus Mosaic
❏ ❏ #2: A Pattern of Blood
❏ ❏ #3: Murder in the Forum
❏ ❏ #4: The Chariots of Calyx
❏ ❏ #5: The Legatus Mystery
❏ ❏ #6: The Ghosts of Glevum
❏ ❏ #7: Enemies of the Empire
❏ ❏ #8: A Roman Ransom
❏ ❏ #9: A Coin for the Ferryman
❏ ❏ #10: Death at Pompeia's Wedding
❏ ❏ # _____

Rowland, Laura Joh

Sano Ichiro: In ancient Japan, Ichiro is a noble samurai and chief investigator.

❏ ❏ #1: Shinju

❑ ❑ #2: Bundori
❑ ❑ #3: The Way of the Traitor
❑ ❑ #4: The Concubine's Tattoo
❑ ❑ #5: The Samurai's Wife
❑ ❑ #6: Black Lotus
❑ ❑ #7: The Pillow Book of Lady Wisteria
❑ ❑ #8: The Dragon King's Palace
❑ ❑ #9: The Perfumed Sleeve
❑ ❑ #10: The Assassin's Touch
❑ ❑ #11: The Red Chrysanthemum
❑ ❑ #12: The Snow Empress
❑ ❑ #13: The Fire Kimono
❑ ❑ #14: The Cloud Pavilion
❑ ❑ # _____

Royal, Priscilla

Prioress Eleanor: During the 13th century, a young
noblewoman becomes Prioress of Tyndal.
❑ ❑ #1: Wine of Violence
❑ ❑ #2: Tyrant of the Mind
❑ ❑ #3: Sorrow Without End
❑ ❑ #4: Justice for the Damned
❑ ❑ #5: Forsaken Soul
❑ ❑ #6: Chambers of Death
❑ ❑ # _____

Rozan, S.J.

Bill Smith/Lydia Chin: Smith and Chin are New York
private eyes who alternate as narrators of the cases they
work together.
❑ ❑ #1: China Trade
❑ ❑ #2: Concourse
❑ ❑ #3: Mandarin Plaid
❑ ❑ #4: No Colder Place

❑ ❑ #5: A Bitter Feast
❑ ❑ #6: Stone Quarry
❑ ❑ #7: Reflecting the Sky
❑ ❑ #8: Winter and Night
❑ ❑ #9: The Shanghai Moon
❑ ❑ # _____

RUCKA, GREG

Atticus Kodiak: Kodiak is a bodyguard who often has
to confront violence on the job.

❑ ❑ #1: Keeper
❑ ❑ #2: Finder
❑ ❑ #3: Smoker
❑ ❑ #4: Shooting at Midnight
❑ ❑ #5: Critical Space
❑ ❑ #6: Patriot Acts
❑ ❑ #7: Walking Dead
❑ ❑ # _____

RYAN, HANK PHILLIPPI

Charlotte McNally: McNally is a star investigative
reporter for a Boston television station.

❑ ❑ #1: Prime Time
❑ ❑ #2: Face Time
❑ ❑ #3: Air Time
❑ ❑ # _____

SANDFORD, JOHN

Kidd: Kidd and LuEllen are con artists who take full
advantage of modern technology.

❑ ❑ #1: The Fool's Run
❑ ❑ #2: The Empress File
❑ ❑ #3: The Devil's Code

❏ ❏ #4: The Hanged Man's Song
❏ ❏ # _____

Lucas Davenport: Police Lieutenant Davenport tracks down some of Minnesota's worst serial killers.
❏ ❏ #1: Rules of Prey
❏ ❏ #2: Shadow Prey
❏ ❏ #3: Eyes of Prey
❏ ❏ #4: Silent Prey
❏ ❏ #5: Winter Prey
❏ ❏ #6: Night Prey
❏ ❏ #7: Mind Prey
❏ ❏ #8: Sudden Prey
❏ ❏ #9: Secret Prey
❏ ❏ #10: Certain Prey
❏ ❏ #11: Easy Prey
❏ ❏ #12: Chosen Prey
❏ ❏ #13: Mortal Prey
❏ ❏ #14: Naked Prey
❏ ❏ #15: Hidden Prey
❏ ❏ #16: Broken Prey
❏ ❏ #17: Invisible Prey
❏ ❏ #18: Phantom Prey
❏ ❏ #19: Wicked Prey
❏ ❏ # _____

SANSOM, C.J.

Matthew Shardlake: In the 16th century, Shardlake works for Thomas Cromwell as a fixer.
❏ ❏ #1: Dissolution
❏ ❏ #2: Dark Fire
❏ ❏ #3: Sovereign

❑ ❑ #4: Revelation
❑ ❑ # _____

SANSOM, IAN

Israel Armstrong: Armstrong runs the mobile library in a small town in Northern Ireland.
❑ ❑ #1: The Case of the Missing Books
❑ ❑ #2: Mr. Dixon Disappears
❑ ❑ #3: The Book Stops Here
❑ ❑ #4: The Bad Book Affair
❑ ❑ # _____

SANTLOFER, JONATHAN

Kate McKinnon: McKinnon traded in her NYPD badge for a Ph.D. in Art History.
❑ ❑ #1: The Death Artist
❑ ❑ #2: Color Blind
❑ ❑ #3: The Killing Art
❑ ❑ # _____

Nate Rodriguez: Rodriguez is a police sketch artist working for the NYPD.
❑ ❑ #1: Anatomy of Fear
❑ ❑ #2: The Murder Notebook
❑ ❑ # _____

SAUMS, MARY

Thistle & Twigg: After the death of her husband, Jane Thistle moves to tiny Tullulah, Alabama, where she meets Phoebe Twigg.
❑ ❑ #1: Thistle and Twigg
❑ ❑ #2: Mighty Old Bones
❑ ❑ # _____

Saylor, Steven

Roma Sub Rosa: Gordianus the Finder who finds murderers in ancient Rome.

- ❏ ❏ #1: Roman Blood
- ❏ ❏ #2: Arms of Nemesis
- ❏ ❏ #3: Catilina's Riddle
- ❏ ❏ #4: The Venus Throw
- ❏ ❏ #5: A Murder on the Appian Way
- ❏ ❏ #6: The House of the Vestals
- ❏ ❏ #7: Rubicon
- ❏ ❏ #8: Last Seen in Massilia
- ❏ ❏ #9: A Mist of Prophecies
- ❏ ❏ #10: The Judgement of Caesar
- ❏ ❏ #11: A Gladiator Dies Only Once
- ❏ ❏ #12: The Triumph of Caesar
- ❏ ❏ # _____

Schreck, Tom

Duffy Dombrowski: Dombrowski works as a social worker, takes care of his basset hound and boxes professionally.

- ❏ ❏ #1: On the Ropes
- ❏ ❏ #2: TKO
- ❏ ❏ #3: Out Cold
- ❏ ❏ # _____

Schweizer, Mark

Hayden Koenig: Police Chief Koenig is working on the next great noir novel, and he leads the Episcopal Church choir in his small North Carolina town.

- ❏ ❏ #1: The Alto Wore Tweed
- ❏ ❏ #2: The Baritone Wore Chiffon
- ❏ ❏ #3: The Tenor Wore Tapshoes

❏ ❏ #4: The Soprano Wore Falsettos
❏ ❏ #5: The Bass Wore Scales
❏ ❏ #6: The Mezzo Wore Mink
❏ ❏ #7: The Diva Wore Diamonds
❏ ❏ # _____

SEDLEY, KATE

Roger the Chapman: In the 15th century, itinerant peddler Roger has an affinity for mysteries.
❏ ❏ #1: Death and the Chapman
❏ ❏ #2: The Plymouth Cloak
❏ ❏ #3: The Weaver's Tale
❏ ❏ #4: The Holy Innocents
❏ ❏ #5: The Eve of Saint Hyacinth
❏ ❏ #6: The Wicked Winter
❏ ❏ #7: The Brothers of Glastonbury
❏ ❏ #8: The Weaver's Inheritance
❏ ❏ #9: The Saint John's Fern
❏ ❏ #10: The Goldsmith's Daughter
❏ ❏ #11: The Lammas Feast
❏ ❏ #12: Nine Men Dancing
❏ ❏ #13: The Midsummer Rose
❏ ❏ #14: The Burgundian's Tale
❏ ❏ #15: The Prodigal Son
❏ ❏ #16: The Three Kings of Cologne
❏ ❏ #17: The Green Man
❏ ❏ #18: The Dance of Death
❏ ❏ # _____

SEFTON, MAGGIE

Kelly Flynn: Before walking into the House of Lambspun in Colorado, Kelly Flynn had never picked up a pair of knitting needles she liked.
❏ ❏ #1: Knit One, Kill Two

❑ ❑ #2: Needled to Death
❑ ❑ #3: A Deadly Yarn
❑ ❑ #4: A Killer Stitch
❑ ❑ #5: Dyer Consequences
❑ ❑ #6: Fleece Navidad
❑ ❑ #7: Dropped Dead Stitch
❑ ❑ # _____

SHANNON, JOHN

Jack Liffey: Liffey lost his job and his family, so now
he searches for missing children in Southern California.
❑ ❑ #1: The Concrete River
❑ ❑ #2: The Cracked Earth
❑ ❑ #3: The Poison Sky
❑ ❑ #4: The Orange Curtain
❑ ❑ #5: Streets on Fire
❑ ❑ #6: City of Strangers
❑ ❑ #7: Terminal Island
❑ ❑ #8: Dangerous Games
❑ ❑ #9: The Dark Streets
❑ ❑ #10: The Devils of Bakersfield
❑ ❑ #11: Palos Verdes Blue
❑ ❑ # _____

SHARP, ZOË

Charlie Fox: Bodyguard Fox specializes in close
protection, working with a colleague from her army
past.
❑ ❑ #1: Killer Instinct
❑ ❑ #2: Riot Act
❑ ❑ #3: Hard Knocks
❑ ❑ #4: First Drop
❑ ❑ #5: Road Kill
❑ ❑ #6: Second Shot

❏ ❏ #7: Third Strike
❏ ❏ # _____

SHORT, SHARON

Josie Toadfern: Toadfern runs a Laundromat in Ohio, where she's a whiz at stain removal.
❏ ❏ #1: Death of a Domestic Diva
❏ ❏ #2: Death by Deep Dish Pie
❏ ❏ #3: Death in the Cards
❏ ❏ #4: Hung Out to Die
❏ ❏ #5: Murder Unfolds
❏ ❏ #6: Tie Dyed and Dead
❏ ❏ # _____

SILVA, DANIEL

Gabriel Allon: Allon wanted to retire from Israeli Intelligence to become an art restorer, but he keeps getting pulled back in to his life of espionage.
❏ ❏ #1: The Kill Artist
❏ ❏ #2: The English Assassin
❏ ❏ #3: The Confessor
❏ ❏ #4: A Death in Vienna
❏ ❏ #5: Prince of Fire
❏ ❏ #6: The Messenger
❏ ❏ #7: The Secret Servant
❏ ❏ #8: Moscow Rules
❏ ❏ #9: The Defector
❏ ❏ # _____

SLAN, JOANNA CAMPBELL

Kiki Lowenstein: Lowenstein loves scrapbooking, her daughter, and solving mysteries.
❏ ❏ #1: Paper, Scissors, Death

- ❏ ❏ #2: Cut, Crop & Die
- ❏ ❏ # _____

SLAUGHTER, KARIN

Grant County: Sara Linton is the medical examiner in Heartsdale, Georgia.
- ❏ ❏ #1: Blindsighted
- ❏ ❏ #2: Kisscut
- ❏ ❏ #3: A Faint Cold Fear
- ❏ ❏ #4: Indelible
- ❏ ❏ #5: Faithless
- ❏ ❏ #6: Beyond Reach
- ❏ ❏ #7: Undone
- ❏ ❏ # _____

Will Trent: Special Agent Trent is a member of the Criminal Apprehension Team stationed in Georgia.
- ❏ ❏ #1: Triptych
- ❏ ❏ #2: Fractured
- ❏ ❏ # _____

SMITH, ALEXANDER MCCALL

Isabel Dalhousie: Dalhousie edits The Review of Applied Ethics in Edinburgh.
- ❏ ❏ #1: The Sunday Philosophy Club
- ❏ ❏ #2: Friends, Lovers, Chocolate
- ❏ ❏ #3: The Right Attitude to Rain
- ❏ ❏ #4: The Careful Use of Compliments
- ❏ ❏ #5: The Comforts of a Muddy Saturday
- ❏ ❏ #6: The Lost Art of Gratitude
- ❏ ❏ # _____

No. 1 Ladies Detective Agency: In Botswana, Precious
Ramotswe is the only (and best) female private
detective.
- ❑ ❑ #1: The No. 1 Ladies' Detective Agency
- ❑ ❑ #2: Tears of the Giraffe
- ❑ ❑ #3: Morality for Beautiful Girls
- ❑ ❑ #4: The Kalahari Typing School for Men
- ❑ ❑ #5: The Full Cupboard of Life
- ❑ ❑ #6: In the Company of Cheerful Ladies
- ❑ ❑ #7: Blue Shoes and Happiness
- ❑ ❑ #8: The Good Husband of Zebra Drive
- ❑ ❑ #9: The Miracle at Speedy Motors
- ❑ ❑ #10: Tea Time for the Traditionally Built
- ❑ ❑ # _____

SPENCER-FLEMING, JULIA

Clare Fergusson: Reverend Fergusson is the new priest
in St. Alban, New York, where she teams up with the
police chief, Russ Van Alstyne.
- ❑ ❑ #1: In the Bleak Midwinter
- ❑ ❑ #2: A Fountain Filled With Blood
- ❑ ❑ #3: Out of the Deep I Cry
- ❑ ❑ #4: To Darkness and to Death
- ❑ ❑ #5: All Mortal Flesh
- ❑ ❑ #6: I Shall Not Want
- ❑ ❑ #7: One Was a Soldier
- ❑ ❑ # _____

SPIEGELMAN, PETER

John March: After a personal tragedy, March left his job
as a deputy sheriff to be a PI in Manhattan.
- ❑ ❑ #1: Black Maps
- ❑ ❑ #2: Death's Little Helpers

❏ ❏   #3: Red Cat
❏ ❏   # _____

SPRINKLE, PATRICIA

Katharine Murray: Atlanta socialite Murray discovers
many mysteries as she investigates her family tree.
❏ ❏   #1: Death on the Family Tree
❏ ❏   #2: Sins of the Fathers
❏ ❏   #3: Daughter of Deceit
❏ ❏   # _____

MacLaren Yarbrough: Magistrate Yarbrough asks the
tough questions in Georgia.
❏ ❏   #1: When Did We Lose Harriet?
❏ ❏   #2: But Why Shoot the Magistrate?
❏ ❏   #3: Who Invited the Dead Man?
❏ ❏   #4: Who Left That Body in the Rain?
❏ ❏   #5: Who Let that Killer in the House?
❏ ❏   #6: When Will the Dead Lady Sing?
❏ ❏   #7: Who Killed the Queen of Clubs?
❏ ❏   #8: Did You Declare the Corpse?
❏ ❏   #9: Guess Who's Coming to Die
❏ ❏   #10: What Are You Wearing To Die?
❏ ❏   # _____

STABENOW, DANA

Kate Shugak: Shugak is a Aleut and an private eye in
Alaska.
❏ ❏   #1: A Cold Day for Murder
❏ ❏   #2: A Fatal Thaw
❏ ❏   #3: Dead in the Water
❏ ❏   #4: A Cold-Blooded Business
❏ ❏   #5: Play With Fire

❏ ❏ #6: Blood Will Tell
❏ ❏ #7: Breakup
❏ ❏ #8: Killing Grounds
❏ ❏ #9: Hunter's Moon
❏ ❏ #10: Midnight Come Again
❏ ❏ #11: The Singing of the Dead
❏ ❏ #12: A Fine and Bitter Snow
❏ ❏ #13: A Grave Denied
❏ ❏ #14: A Taint in the Blood
❏ ❏ #15: A Deeper Sleep
❏ ❏ #16: Whisper to the Blood
❏ ❏ # _____

STANLEY, J.B.

Supper Club: James "Professor Puff" Henry wants to avoid carbs and lose weight.

❏ ❏ #1: Carbs & Cadavers
❏ ❏ #2: Fit to Die
❏ ❏ #3: Chili Con Corpses
❏ ❏ #4: Stiffs and Swine
❏ ❏ #5: The Battered Body
❏ ❏ # _____

STRALEY, JOHN

Cecil Younger: Younger is an alcoholic private eye who investigates crimes in the Alaskan frontier.

❏ ❏ #1: The Woman Who Married a Bear
❏ ❏ #2: The Curious Eat Themselves
❏ ❏ #3: The Music of What Happens
❏ ❏ #4: Death and the Language of Happiness
❏ ❏ #5: The Angels Will Not Care
❏ ❏ #6: Cold Water Burning
❏ ❏ # _____

SWANSON, DENISE

Skye Denison: Denison tried to leave the small Illinois town of Scumble River years ago but now she's back, working as a school psychologist.

- ❏ ❏ #1: Murder of a Small-Town Honey
- ❏ ❏ #2: Murder of a Sweet Old Lady
- ❏ ❏ #3: Murder of a Sleeping Beauty
- ❏ ❏ #4: Murder of a Snake in the Grass
- ❏ ❏ #5: Murder of a Barbie and Ken
- ❏ ❏ #6: Murder of a Pink Elephant
- ❏ ❏ #7: Murder of a Smart Cookie
- ❏ ❏ #8: Murder of a Real Bad Boy
- ❏ ❏ #9: Murder of a Botoxed Blonde
- ❏ ❏ #10: Murder of a Chocolate-Covered Cherry
- ❏ ❏ #11: Murder of a Royal Pain
- ❏ ❏ # _____

TAICHERT, PARI NOSKIN

Sasha Solomon: Solomon is a PR director who gets into some of the weirdest stuff in New Mexico.

- ❏ ❏ #1: The Clovis Incident
- ❏ ❏ #2: The Belen Hitch
- ❏ ❏ #3: The Socorro Blast
- ❏ ❏ # _____

TALLEY, MARCIA

Hannah Ives: Breast cancer survivor Ives gets involved in mysteries in Maryland.

- ❏ ❏ #1: Sing It to Her Bones
- ❏ ❏ #2: Unbreathed Memories
- ❏ ❏ #3: Occasion of Revenge
- ❏ ❏ #4: In Death's Shadow
- ❏ ❏ #5: This Enemy Town

❏ ❏ #6: Through the Darkness
❏ ❏ #7: Dead Man Dancing
❏ ❏ #8: Without a Grave
❏ ❏ # _____

TAPPLY, WILLIAM G.

Brady Coyne: Boston attorney Coyne's clients are well-off, and consult him on more than just legal issues.
❏ ❏ #1: Death at Charity's Point
❏ ❏ #2: The Dutch Blue Error
❏ ❏ #3: Follow the Sharks
❏ ❏ #4: The Marine Corpse
❏ ❏ #5: Dead Meat
❏ ❏ #6: The Vulgar Boatman
❏ ❏ #7: A Void in Hearts
❏ ❏ #8: Dead Winter
❏ ❏ #9: Client Privilege
❏ ❏ #10: The Spotted Cats
❏ ❏ #11: Tight Lines
❏ ❏ #12: The Snake Eater
❏ ❏ #13: The Seventh Enemy
❏ ❏ #14: Close to the Bone
❏ ❏ #15: Cutter's Run
❏ ❏ #16: Muscle Memory
❏ ❏ #17: Scar Tissue
❏ ❏ #18: Past Tense
❏ ❏ #19: A Fine Line
❏ ❏ #20: Shadow of Death
❏ ❏ #21: Nervous Water
❏ ❏ #22: Out Cold
❏ ❏ #23: One-Way Ticket
❏ ❏ #24: Hell Bent
❏ ❏ # _____

TAYLOR, SARAH STEWART

Sweeney St. George: St. George is a Harvard University professor who specializes in funeral art.

❏ ❏ #1: O' Artful Death
❏ ❏ #2: Mansions of the Dead
❏ ❏ #3: Judgment of the Grave
❏ ❏ #4: Still as Death
❏ ❏ # _____

THAYER, TERRI

Dewey Pellicano: Pellicano inherits a store for quilters.

❏ ❏ #1: Wild Goose Chase
❏ ❏ #2: Old Maid's Puzzle
❏ ❏ #3: Ocean Waves
❏ ❏ # _____

Stamping Sisters: April Buchert is a professional rubber stamper in Pennsylvania.

❏ ❏ #1: Stamped Out
❏ ❏ #2: Inked Up
❏ ❏ # _____

THOMAS, WILL

Barker & Llewelyn: On the streets of Victorian London, detective Cyrus Barker and his assistant Thomas Llewelyn disentangle gruesome murders.

❏ ❏ #1: Some Danger Involved
❏ ❏ #2: To Kingdom Come
❏ ❏ #3: The Limehouse Text
❏ ❏ #4: The Hellfire Conspiracy
❏ ❏ #5: The Black Hand
❏ ❏ # _____

THOMPSON, VICTORIA

Gaslight Mysteries: Midwife Sarah Brandt teams up
with Sergeant Frank Malloy to find killers on the streets
of turn-of-the-century New York.

- ❏ ❏ #1: Murder on Astor Place
- ❏ ❏ #2: Murder on St. Mark's Place
- ❏ ❏ #3: Murder on Gramercy Park
- ❏ ❏ #4: Murder on Washington Square
- ❏ ❏ #5: Murder on Mulberry Bend
- ❏ ❏ #6: Murder on Marble Row
- ❏ ❏ #7: Murder on Lenox Hill
- ❏ ❏ #8: Murder in Little Italy
- ❏ ❏ #9: Murder in Chinatown
- ❏ ❏ #10: Murder on Bank Street
- ❏ ❏ #11: Murder on Waverly Place
- ❏ ❏ # _____

THURLO, AIMÉE & DAVID

Ella Clah: Clah is a Navajo FBI agent who uses modern
and ancient techniques to get to the bottom of crimes.

- ❏ ❏ #1: Blackening Song
- ❏ ❏ #2: Death Walker
- ❏ ❏ #3: Bad Medicine
- ❏ ❏ #4: Enemy Way
- ❏ ❏ #5: Shooting Chant
- ❏ ❏ #6: Red Mesa
- ❏ ❏ #7: Changing Woman
- ❏ ❏ #8: Plant Them Deep
- ❏ ❏ #9: Tracking Bear
- ❏ ❏ #10: Wind Spirit
- ❏ ❏ #11: White Thunder
- ❏ ❏ #12: Mourning Dove
- ❏ ❏ #13: Turquoise Girl
- ❏ ❏ #14: Coyote's Wife

❏ ❏ #15: Earthway

❏ ❏ # _____

Sister Agatha: Our Lady of Hope Sister Agatha has her
faith tested when she solves murders in New Mexico.

❏ ❏ #1: Bad Faith
❏ ❏ #2: Thief in Retreat
❏ ❏ #3: Prey for a Miracle
❏ ❏ #4: False Witness
❏ ❏ #5: The Prodigal Nun
❏ ❏ #6: Bad Samaritan
❏ ❏ # _____

TIERNEY, RONALD

Deets Shanahan: Shanahan is a private detective in his
70s who still investigates mysteries in Indianapolis.

❏ ❏ #1: The Stone Veil
❏ ❏ #2: The Steel Web
❏ ❏ #3: The Iron Glove
❏ ❏ #4: The Concrete Pillow
❏ ❏ #5: Nickel-Plated Soul
❏ ❏ #6: Platinum Canary
❏ ❏ #7: Glass Chameleon
❏ ❏ #8: Asphalt Moon
❏ ❏ #9: Bloody Palms
❏ ❏ # _____

TODD, CHARLES

Ian Rutledge: After World War I, Rutledge returns to
Scotland Yard haunted by the war.

❏ ❏ #1: A Test of Wills
❏ ❏ #2: Wings of Fire
❏ ❏ #3: Search the Dark

❏ ❏ #4: Legacy of the Dead
❏ ❏ #5: Watchers of Time
❏ ❏ #6: A Fearsome Doubt
❏ ❏ #7: A Cold Treachery
❏ ❏ #8: A Long Shadow
❏ ❏ #9: A False Mirror
❏ ❏ #10: A Pale Horse
❏ ❏ #11: A Matter of Justice
❏ ❏ # _____

TOOLEY, S.D.

Sam Casey: Detective Sergeant Casey has the unique ability to talk to the dead.
❏ ❏ #1: When the Dead Speak
❏ ❏ #2: Nothing Else Matters
❏ ❏ #3: Restless Spirit
❏ ❏ #4: Echoes from the Grave
❏ ❏ # _____

TRACY, P.J.

Grace McBride: McBride runs Monkeewrench, a software company in Minneapolis.
❏ ❏ #1: Monkeewrench
❏ ❏ #2: Live Bait
❏ ❏ #3: Dead Run
❏ ❏ #4: Snow Blind
❏ ❏ # _____

TREMAYNE, PETER

Sister Fidelma: In the first century A.D., Sister Fidelma of the Celtic Church investigates mysteries.
❏ ❏ #1: Absolution by Murder
❏ ❏ #2: Shroud for the Archbishop

VIETS, ELAINE

Helen Hawthorne: Hawthorne works in one menial job after another in an effort to live her life under the radar.

Josie Marcus: Marcus is a mystery shopper in St. Louis.
- ❏ ❏ #1: Dying in Style
- ❏ ❏ #2: High Heels Are Murder
- ❏ ❏ #3: An Accessory to Murder
- ❏ ❏ #4: Murder With All the Trimmings
- ❏ ❏ #5: The Fashion Hound Murders
- ❏ ❏ # _____

WALL, KATHRYN R.

Bay Tanner: Tanner is a financial consultant and a recent widow in South Carolina.
- ❏ ❏ #1: In for a Penny
- ❏ ❏ #2: And Not a Penny More
- ❏ ❏ #3: Perdition House
- ❏ ❏ #4: Judas Island
- ❏ ❏ #5: Resurrection Road
- ❏ ❏ #6: Bishop's Reach
- ❏ ❏ #7: Sanctuary Hill
- ❏ ❏ #8: The Mercy Oak
- ❏ ❏ #9: Covenant Hall
- ❏ ❏ # _____

WEBBER, HEATHER

Nina Quinn: Quinn's landscaping firm specializes in surprise garden makeovers.
- ❏ ❏ #1: A Hoe Lot of Trouble
- ❏ ❏ #2: Trouble in Spades
- ❏ ❏ #3: Digging Up Trouble
- ❏ ❏ #4: Trouble in Bloom
- ❏ ❏ #5: Weeding Out Trouble
- ❏ ❏ # _____

WHITE, RANDY WAYNE

Doc Ford: Ford works as a marine biologist on Florida's Gulf Coast. He's also a retired NSA agent.

- ❏ ❏ #1: Sanibel Flats
- ❏ ❏ #2: The Heat Islands
- ❏ ❏ #3: The Man Who Invented Florida
- ❏ ❏ #4: Captiva
- ❏ ❏ #5: North of Havana
- ❏ ❏ #6: The Mangrove Coast
- ❏ ❏ #7: Ten Thousand Islands
- ❏ ❏ #8: Shark River
- ❏ ❏ #9: Twelve Mile Limit
- ❏ ❏ #10: Everglades
- ❏ ❏ #11: Tampa Burn
- ❏ ❏ #12: Dead of Night
- ❏ ❏ #13: Dark Light
- ❏ ❏ #14: Hunter's Moon
- ❏ ❏ #15: Black Widow
- ❏ ❏ #16: Dead Silence
- ❏ ❏ #17: Deep Shadow
- ❏ ❏ # _____

WILSON, ROBERT

Javier Falcon: Falcon is a homicide detective working in Seville who deals with intensely psychological crimes.

- ❏ ❏ #1: The Blind Man of Seville
- ❏ ❏ #2: The Vanished Hands
- ❏ ❏ #3: The Hidden Assassins
- ❏ ❏ #4: The Ignorance of Blood
- ❏ ❏ # _____

Winspear, Jacqueline

Maisie Dobbs: Dobbs was a nurse during World War I, and is now a private detective in London.
- ❏ ❏ #1: Maisie Dobbs
- ❏ ❏ #2: Birds of a Feather
- ❏ ❏ #3: Pardonable Lies
- ❏ ❏ #4: Messenger of Truth
- ❏ ❏ #5: An Incomplete Revenge
- ❏ ❏ #6: Among the Mad
- ❏ ❏ # _____

Wishart, David

Marcus Corvinus: In Ancient Rome, Corvinus has a taste for solving crimes.
- ❏ ❏ #1: Ovid
- ❏ ❏ #2: Germanicus
- ❏ ❏ #3: The Lydian Baker
- ❏ ❏ #4: Sejanus
- ❏ ❏ #5: Old Bones
- ❏ ❏ #6: Last Rites
- ❏ ❏ #7: White Murder
- ❏ ❏ #8: A Vote for Murder
- ❏ ❏ #9: Parthian Shot
- ❏ ❏ #10: Food for the Fishes
- ❏ ❏ #11: In at the Death
- ❏ ❏ #12: Illegally Dead
- ❏ ❏ # _____

Woods, Stuart

Holly Barker: Ex-Army major Barker is now the deputy chief of police in Orchid Beach, Florida.
- ❏ ❏ #1: Orchid Beach
- ❏ ❏ #2: Orchid Blues

❏ ❏ #3: Blood Orchid
❏ ❏ #4: Reckless Abandon
❏ ❏ #5: Iron Orchid
❏ ❏ #6: Hothouse Orchid
❏ ❏ # _____

Stone Barrington: Detective Sergeant Barrington works in New York City.
❏ ❏ #1: New York Dead
❏ ❏ #2: Dirt
❏ ❏ #3: Dead in the Water
❏ ❏ #4: Swimming To Catalina
❏ ❏ #5: Worst Fears Realized
❏ ❏ #6: L.A. Dead
❏ ❏ #7: Cold Paradise
❏ ❏ #8: The Short Forever
❏ ❏ #9: Dirty Work
❏ ❏ #10: Reckless Abandon
❏ ❏ #11: Two Dollar Bill
❏ ❏ #12: Dark Harbor
❏ ❏ #13: Fresh Disasters
❏ ❏ #14: Shoot Him If He Runs
❏ ❏ #15: Hot Mahogany
❏ ❏ #16: Loitering with Intent
❏ ❏ #17: Kisser
❏ ❏ # _____

Will Lee: This epic series spans several generations of Police Chief Lee's family.
❏ ❏ #1: Chiefs
❏ ❏ #2: Run Before the Wind
❏ ❏ #3: Deep Lie
❏ ❏ #4: Grass Roots
❏ ❏ #5: The Run

❏ ❏ #6: Capital Crimes
❏ ❏ #7: Mounting Fears
❏ ❏ # _____

WRIGHT, EDWARD

John Ray Horn: Horn used to be an actor in Westerns, he's blacklisted after a stint in prison.
❏ ❏ #1: Clea's Moon
❏ ❏ #2: While I Disappear
❏ ❏ #3: Red Sky Lament
❏ ❏ # _____

WRIGHT, SALLY

Ben Reese: Reese is a university archivist who was a World War II scout.
❏ ❏ #1: Publish and Perish
❏ ❏ #2: Pride and Predator
❏ ❏ #3: Pursuit and Persuasion
❏ ❏ #4: Out of the Ruins
❏ ❏ #5: Watches of the Night
❏ ❏ #6: Code of Silence
❏ ❏ # _____

XIAOLONG, QIU

Inspector Chen: Inspector Chen Cao works in the Shanghai Police Bureau. He often teams with US Marshal Catherine Rohn to solve cases.
❏ ❏ #1: Death of a Red Heroine
❏ ❏ #2: A Loyal Character Dancer
❏ ❏ #3: When Red Is Black
❏ ❏ #4: A Case of Two Cities
❏ ❏ #5: Red Mandarin Dress

❏ ❏ #6: The Mao Case

❏ ❏ # _____

ZUBRO, MARK RICHARD

Paul Turner: Gay police detective Turner works in Chicago while still being a single father.

❏ ❏ #1: Sorry Now?
❏ ❏ #2: Political Poison
❏ ❏ #3: Another Dead Teenager
❏ ❏ #4: The Truth Can Get You Killed
❏ ❏ #5: Drop Dead
❏ ❏ #6: Sex and Murder.com
❏ ❏ #7: Dead Egotistical Morons
❏ ❏ #8: Nerds Who Kill
❏ ❏ #9: Hook Line and Homicide
❏ ❏ # _____

Mason & Carpenter: High school teacher Tom Mason is in a relationship with professional baseball player Scott Carpenter.

❏ ❏ #1: A Simple Suburban Murder
❏ ❏ #2: Why Isn't Becky Twitchell Dead?
❏ ❏ #3: The Only Good Priest
❏ ❏ #4: The Principal Cause of Death
❏ ❏ #5: An Echo of Death
❏ ❏ #6: Rust on the Razor
❏ ❏ #7: Are You Nuts?
❏ ❏ #8: One Dead Drag Queen
❏ ❏ #9: Here Comes the Corpse
❏ ❏ #10: File Under Dead
❏ ❏ #11: Everyone's Dead But Us
❏ ❏ #12: Schooled in Murder
❏ ❏ # _____

"Five great" lists

Lists, for lack of a better word, are fun. They're fun to debate, to create and to read. We have created a set of lists featuring series that are in this book that will might help you find new series that will become your favorites.

Five Great...

Cat Related Mysteries
1. Cat Who...series by Lilian Jackson Braun
2. Mrs. Murphy series by Rita Mae Brown
3. Cat Marsala series by Barbara D'Amato
4. Midnight Louie series by Carole Nelson Douglas
5. Joe Grey series by Shirley Rousseau Murphy

Celebrity Detectives
1. Beatrix Potter series by Susan Wittig Albert (Beatrix Potter)
2. Jane Austen series by Stephanie Barron (Jane Austen)
3. Mr. and Mrs. Darcy series by Carrie A. Bebris (Mr. and Mrs. Darcy)
4. Oscar Wilde series by Gyles Brandreth (Oscar Wilde)
5. Mary Russell series by Laurie R. King (Sherlock Holmes)

Cheerful Mysteries
1. Dorothy Martin series by Jeanne M. Dams
2. Lucy Stone series by Leslie Meier
3. Faith Fairchild series by Katherine Hall Page
4. Three Pines series by Louise Penny
5. MacLaren Yarbrough series by Patricia Sprinkle

Chicago Mysteries
1. Ron Shade series by Michael A. Black
2. Ray Dudgeon series by Sean Chercover
3. Georgia Davis series by Libby Fischer Hellmann
4. V.I. Warshawski series by Sara Paretsky
5. Paul Turner series by Mark Richard Zubro

Craft Related Mysteries
1. Needlecraft series by Monica Ferris
2. Crochet series by Betty Hechtman
3. Knitting series by Maggie Sefton
4. Snap-N-Craft series by Joanna Campbell Slan
5. Quilting series by Terri Thayer

Detective Inspector Mysteries
1. C.D. Sloan series by Catherine Aird
2. Cooper and Fry series by Stephen Booth
3. Inspector Lynley series by Elizabeth George
4. Dalziel and Pascoe series by Reginald Hill
5. Alan Banks series by Peter Robinson

Dog Related Mysteries
1. Yooper series by Deb Baker
2. Mrs. Murphy series by Rita Mae Brown
3. Dixie Hemingway series by Blaize Clement
4. Andy Carpenter series by David Rosenfelt
5. Duffy Dombrowski series by Tom Schreck

Exotic Locations in Mysteries
1. Jade del Cameron series by Suzanne Arruda (Africa)
2. Joe Sandilands series by Barbara Cleverly (India)
3. Dr. Siri series by Colin Cotterill (Laos)
4. Mario Silva series by Leighton Gage
5. Detective Erlendur series by Arnaldur Indridason (Iceland)

Florida Mysteries
1. Stuff series by Don Bruns
2. Serge A. Storms series by Tim Dorsey
3. Lew Fonesca series by Stuart M. Kaminsky
4. Louis Kincaid series by P.J. Parrish
5. Doc Ford series by Randy Wayne White

"Fixers"
1. Jonathan Quinn series by Brett Battles
2. Jack Reacher series by Lee Child
3. Volk series by Brent Ghelfi
4. Fool's Guild series by Alan Gordon
5. Bangkok series by Timothy Hallinan

Forensic Mysteries
1. Kay Scarpetta series by Patricia Cornwell
2. Lincoln Rhyme series by Jeffery Deaver
3. Rizzoli/Isles series by Tess Gerritsen
4. Eve Duncan series by Iris Johansen
5. Temperance Brennan series by Kathy Reichs

Funny Mysteries
1. Meg Langslow series by Donna Andrews
2. Myron Bolitar series by Harlan Coben
3. Fool's Guild series by Alan Gordon
4. Puzzle Lady series by Parnell Hall
5. Jaine Austen series by Laura Levine

Gory Mysteries
1. Lincoln Rhyme series by Jeffery Deaver
2. Jack Daniels series by J.A. Konrath
3. Dexter Morgan series by Jeff Lindsay
4. Alex Cross series by James Patterson
5. Lucas Davenport series by John Sandford

Indiana Mysteries
1. Hilda Johansson series by Jeanne M. Dams
2. Colton Parker series by Brandt Dodson
3. Albert Samson series by Michael Z. Lewin
4. Nick Bertetto series by Tony Perona
5. Deets Shanahan series by Ronald Tierney

Irregular Mysteries
1. Thursday Next series by Jasper Fforde
2. Brant and May series by Christopher Fowler
3. Dalziel and Pascoe series by Reginald Hill
4. Peter Diamond series by Peter Lovesey
5. Sasha Solomon series by Pari Noskin Taichert

L.A. Mysteries
1. Harry Bosch series by Michael Connelly
2. Elvis Cole series by Robert Crais
3. Mas Arai series by Naomi Hirahara
4. Peter Decker series by Faye Kellerman
5. Alex Delaware series by Jonathan Kellerman

Legal Thrillers
1. Ben Kincaid series by William Bernhardt
2. Mickey Haller series by Michael Connelly
3. Steve Winslow series by J.P. Hailey
4. Dismas Hardy series by John Lescroart
5. Solomon vs. Lord series by Paul Levine

Medieval England Mysteries
1. Hawkenlye series by Alys Clare
2. Sister Frevisse series by Margaret Frazer
3. Medieval West Country series by Michael Jecks
4. Crowner John series by Bernard Knight
5. Owen Archer series by Candace Robb

Medieval Elsewhere Mysteries
1. Fool's Guild series by Alan Gordon (Europe)
2. Gilbert Cunningham series by Pat McIntosh (Scotland)
3. Catherine LeVendeur series by Sharan Newman (France)
4. Sano Ichiro series by Laura Joh Rowland (Japan)
5. Sister Fidelma series by Peter Tremayne (Ireland)

Names of Protagonists
1. U.S. Marshal Piedmont Kelly series by Phil Dunlap
2. Tess Monaghan series by Laura Lippman
3. Charlie Fox series by Zoë Sharp
4. Gabriel Allon series by Daniel Silva
5. Deets Shanahan series by Ronald Tierney

Native American Mysteries
1. Father John series by Margaret Coel
2. Charlie Moon series by James D. Doss
3. Jane Whitefield series by Thomas Perry
4. Cecil Younger series by John Straley
5. Ella Clah series by Aimée & David Thurlo

New Jersey Mysteries
1. Myron Bolitar series by Harlan Coben
2. Double Feature series by Jeffrey Cohen
3. Stephanie Plum series by Janet Evanovich

4. John Ceepak series by Chris Grabenstein
5. Andy Carpenter series by David Rosenfelt

New York Mysteries
1. Moe Prager series by Reed Farrel Coleman
2. Kathleen Mallory series by Carol O'Connell
3. Pendergast series by Douglas Preston & Lincoln Child
4. Bill Smith/Lydia Chin series by S.J. Rozan
5. Gaslight Mysteries by Victoria Thompson

No-Nonsense Private Eye Mysteries
1. Amos Walker series by Loren D. Estleman
2. Mac McKenzie series by David Housewright
3. Lincoln Perry series by Michael Koryta
4. Sharon McCone series by Marcia Muller
5. Nameless Detective series by Bill Pronzini

Odes to Literature
1. Booktown Mysteries by Lorna Barrett
2. Cliff Janeway series by John Dunning
3. Thursday Next series by Jasper Fforde
4. Death on Demand series by Carolyn G. Hart
5. Holmes on the Range series by Steve Hockensmith

Paranormal Mysteries
1. Bewitching Mysteries by Madelyn Alt
2. The Dresden Files by Jim Butcher
3. Ophelia and Abby series by Shirley Damsgaard
4. Sookie Stackhouse series by Charlaine Harris
5. Ghost Hunter series by Victoria Laurie

Police Procedurals
1. John Cardinal series by Giles Blunt
2. Dave Robicheaux series by James Lee Burke
3. George Sueno series by Martin Limón
4. Brock and Kolla series by Barry Maitland
5. Joe Gunther series by Archer Mayor

Print Journalism Mysteries
1. Hallie Ahern series by Jan Brogan
2. Irene Kelly series by Jan Burke
3. Emma Lord series by Mary Daheim
4. Cat Marsala series by Barbara D'Amato
5. Henrie O series by Carolyn G. Hart

Roman Empire Mysteries
1. Marcus Didius Falco series by Lindsey Davis
2. Gaius Petreius Ruso series by Ruth Downie
3. Libertus series by Rosemary Rowe
4. Roma Sub Rosa series by Steven Saylor
5. Marcus Corvinus series by David Wishart

Roaring Twenties Mysteries
1. Jade del Cameron series by Suzanne Arruda
2. Her Royal Spyness series by Rhys Bowen
3. Laetitia Talbot series by Barbara Cleverly
4. Daisy Dairymple series by Carola Dunn
5. Phryne Fisher series by Kerry Greenwood

Series for Film Buffs
1. Double Feature series by Jeffrey Cohen
2. Valentino series by Loren D. Estleman
3. Scott Elliot series by Terence Faherty
4. Toby Peters series by Stuart Kaminsky
5. John Ray Horn series by Edward Wright

Series in the Tradition of Agatha Christie
1. Josie Prescott series by Jane K. Cleland
2. Inspector Barnaby series by Caroline Graham
3. Death on Demand series by Carolyn G. Hart
4. Three Pines series by Louise Penny
5. Faith Fairchild series by Katherine Hall Page

Series in the Tradition of Raymond Chandler
1. Ray Dudgeon series by Sean Chercover
2. Elvis Cole series by Robert Crais
3. Amos Walker series by Loren D. Estleman
4. Lincoln Perry series by Michael Koryta
5. Brady Coyne series by William G. Tapply

Series That Had a Cinematic Adapation
1. Bernie Rhodenbarr series by Lawrence Block (*Burglar*)
2. Lincoln Rhyme series by Jeffery Deaver (*The Bone Collector*)
3. Patrick Kenzie series by Dennis Lehand (*Gone, Baby, Gone*)
4. Easy Rawlins series by Walter Mosley (*Devil in a Blue Dress*)
5. V.I. Warshawski series by Sara Paretsky (*V.I. Warshawski*)

Series with Antiques and Collectables
1. Dolls to Die For series by Deb Baker (Dolls)
2. Josie Prescott series by Jane K. Cleland (Antiques)
3. Cliff Janeway series by John Dunning (Books)
4. Jane Wheel series by Sharon Fiffer (Antiques)
5. Bear Collectors series by John J. Lamb (Teddy Bears)

Series in Corrupt Locales
1. Dr. Siri series by Colin Cotterill
2. Mario Silva series by Leighton Gage
3. Volk series by Brent Ghelfi
4. Bangkok series by Timothy Hallinan
5. Guido Brunetti series by Donna Leon

Series with Morally Questionable Protagonists
1. Quarry series by Max Allan Collins
2. Serge A. Storms series by Tim Dorsey
3. John Rain series by Barry Eisler
4. Dexter Morgan series by Jeff Lindsay
5. Atticus Kodiak series by Greg Rucka

Series with Older Protagonists
1. Bryant and May series by Christoper Fowler
2. Puzzle Lady series by Parnell Hall
3. Mas Arai series by Naomi Hirahara
4. Thistle & Twigg series by Mary Saums
5. Deets Shanahan series by Ronald Tierney

Series with Recipes
1. Aunt Dimity series by Nancy Atherton
2. Tea Shop series by Laura Childs
3. Goldy Schultz series by Diane Mott Davidson
4. Hannah Swensen series by Joanne Fluke
5. White House Chef series by Julie Hyzy

Spiritual Mysteries
1. Father John series by Margaret Coel
2. Colton Parker series by Brandt Dodson
3. Owen Keane series by Terence Faherty
4. Catherine LeVendeur series by Sharan Newman
5. Reverend Clare Fergusson series by Julia Spencer-Fleming

Towns We Want to Live in Despite All the Murders
1. Aunt Dimity series by Nancy Atherton (Finch, England)
2. Chocoholic Mysteries by JoAnna Carl (Warner Pier, Michigan)
3. Lucy Stone series by Leslie Meier (Tinker's Cover, Maine)
4. Faith Fairchild series by Katherine Hall Page (Aleford, Massachusetts)
5. Three Pines series by Louise Penny (Three Pines, Canada)

Westerns
1. Joe Pickett series by C.J. Box
2. U.S. Marshal Piedmont Kelly series by Phil Dunlap
3. Holmes on the Range series by Steve Hockensmith
4. Walt Longmire series by Craig Johnson
5. Virgil Cole series by Robert B. Parker

The Mystery Company is an independent bookstore
located in Carmel, Indiana, that specializes in the
mystery genre.

For more information, visit:
www.themysterycompany.com